Robert Nozick

Series Introduction

The *Major Conservative and Libertarian Thinkers* series aims to show that there is a rigorous, scholarly tradition of social and political thought that may be broadly described as 'conservative', 'libertarian' or some combination of the two.

The series aims to show that conservatism is not simply a reaction against contemporary events, nor a privileging of intuitive thought over deductive reasoning; libertarianism is not simply an apology for unfettered capitalism or an attempt to justify a misguided atomistic concept of the individual. Rather, the thinkers in this series have developed coherent intellectual positions that are grounded in empirical reality and also founded upon serious philosophical reflection on the relationship between the individual and society, how the social institutions necessary for a free society are to be established and maintained, and the implications of the limits to human knowledge and certainty.

Each volume in the series presents a thinker's ideas in an accessible and cogent manner to provide an indispensable work for both students with varying degrees of familiarity with the topic as well as more advanced scholars.

The following 20 volumes that make up the entire *Major Conservative and Libertarian Thinkers* series are written by international scholars and experts:

The Salamanca School	Andre Azevedo Alves and José Manuel Moreira
Thomas Hobbes	R. E. R. Bunce
John Locke	Eric Mack
David Hume	Christopher J. Berry
Adam Smith	James Otteson
Edmund Burke	Dennis O'Keeffe
Alexis de Tocqueville	Alan S. Kahan
Herbert Spencer	Alberto Mingardi
Ludwig von Mises	Richard Ebeling
Joseph A. Schumpeter	John Medearis

F. A. Hayek	Adam Tebble
Michael Oakeshott	Edmund Neill
Karl Popper	Philip Parvin
Ayn Rand	Mimi Gladstein
Milton Friedman	William Ruger
Russell Kirk	John Pafford
James M. Buchanan	John Meadowcroft
The Modern Papacy	Samuel Gregg
Murray Rothbard	Gerard Casey
Robert Nozick	Ralf Bader

Of course, in any series of this nature, choices have to be made as to which thinkers to include and which to leave out. Two of the thinkers in the series – F. A. Hayek and James M. Buchanan – have written explicit statements rejecting the label 'conservative'. Similarly, other thinkers, such as David Hume and Karl Popper, may be more accurately described as classical liberals than either conservatives or libertarians. However, these thinkers have been included because a full appreciation of this particular tradition of thought would be impossible without their inclusion; conservative and libertarian thought cannot be fully understood without some knowledge of the intellectual contributions of Hume, Hayek, Popper and Buchanan, among others. Although no list of conservative and libertarian thinkers can be perfect, it is hoped that the volumes in this series come as close as possible to providing a comprehensive account of the key contributors to this particular tradition.

John Meadowcroft
King's College London

Robert Nozick

Ralf M. Bader

Major Conservative and Libertarian Thinkers

Series Editor: John Meadowcroft

BLOOMSBURY

NEW YORK • LONDON • NEW DELHI • SYDNEY

Bloomsbury Academic
An imprint of Bloomsbury Publishing Plc

1385 Broadway	50 Bedford Square
New York	London
NY 10018	WC1B 3DP
USA	UK

www.bloomsbury.com

Hardback edition first published in 2010 by the Continuum
International Publishing Group Inc.

This paperback edition published by Bloomsbury Academic 2013

Library of Congress Cataloging-in-Publication Data
A catalog record for this book is available from the Library of Congress.

ISBN: HB: 978-0-8264-2429-7
     PB: 978-1-4411-8009-4
  ePub: 978-1-6235-6573-2

Typeset by Newgen Imaging Systems Pvt Ltd, Chennai, India
Printed and bound in the United States of America

To my brother

Contents

Acknowledgements

For helpful comments, criticisms and suggestions, I would like to thank Andrew Buchan, Asher Dresner, Chris Freiman, Dan Halliday and John Meadowcroft. I would also like to express my gratitude to Nigel Ashford, Elaine Hawley and the IHS for all their help and support.

Series Editor's Preface

In the second half of the twentieth century libertarian and conservative ideas enjoyed an enormous resurgence. The fact that twelve of the twenty subjects in this series published their major works after 1940 is evidence of this revival. No thinker contributed more to this development than the Harvard philosopher Robert Nozick. Nozick's book *Anarchy, State, and Utopia* moved libertarianism from a relatively neglected subset of political philosophy to the centre of the discipline as one of the most cogent critiques of social democracy and egalitarian liberalism. Indeed, the publication of *Anarchy, State, and Utopia* in 1974, along with the publication of John Rawls' *A Theory of Justice* in 1971, is widely credited with revitalizing the discipline of political theory which many scholars felt had become stale and largely detached from real world concerns of policy and politics.

In this outstanding volume Ralf M. Bader of the University of St Andrews shows why Nozick's *Anarchy, State, and Utopia* proved to be so important and so influential. In *Anarchy, State, and Utopia*, Nozick developed a rights-based account of libertarianism to show that a minimal state can legitimately arise, that nothing more than a minimal state is justified, and that the minimal state is not only morally right but can also be an inspiring 'meta-utopia'. It was in particular the second part of *Anarchy, State, and Utopia*,

written as a response to Rawls' similarly groundbreaking
A Theory of Justice, that turned out to have a lasting impact
on political philosophy. There, Nozick argued that justice
could only ever be procedural and any attempt to achieve
a particular pattern of distribution must infringe people's
basic rights to dispose of their justly-acquired resources as
they saw fit. Nozick used the memorable example of the
wealth acquired by the basketball player Wilt Chamberlain
in a fictional scenario to illustrate his 'entitlement theory
of justice', showing how Chamberlain had acquired his
wealth via a series of just steps and that therefore his new
wealth (and the new overall distribution of wealth) must
be considered just.

By setting out Nozick's thought in an extremely lucid and
accessible manner, this volume makes a crucial contribution to the *Major Conservative and Libertarian Thinkers* series.
It presents Nozick's contributions to political philosophy
in the context of his work in analytical philosophy. It also
provides a biography of Nozick and considers the initial
reception and long-term influence of his work. Certainly no
account of libertarian thought would be complete without
a thorough treatment of the contribution made by Nozick.
This volume will prove indispensable to those relatively
unfamiliar with Nozick's work as well as more advanced
scholars.

John Meadowcroft
King's College London

Note on Citation

Unless otherwise indicated, all citations refer to Robert Nozick's *Anarchy, State, and Utopia* (Nozick: 1974).

1

Biography

Nozick's life

Robert Nozick was born on 16 November 1938 in Brooklyn, the son of a Russian Jewish immigrant family. He became interested in philosophy as an undergraduate at Columbia. In particular, it was as a result of taking an introductory course on Western Civilization by Syndney Morgenbesser that Nozick began to be seriously engaged with philosophy. Morgenbesser was a highly respected philosopher who was well known for his wit and sharp criticism. He did not publish very much, but had a huge impact on his students. Nozick was fascinated by Sydney Morgenbesser and greatly admired his skill in finding problems and dealing with philosophical issues. Nozick attended as many courses by Morgenbesser as possible and described his degree as a 'major in Morgenbesser'.

After completing his degree at Columbia in 1959, Nozick went to Princeton for graduate studies. There, he received his M.A. in 1961 and completed his Ph.D. in 1963 under the supervision of Carl Hempel. Hempel was a famous German philosopher of science and an important advocate of logical empiricism. Nozick's dissertation, *The Normative Theory of Individual Choice*, is a technical work which deals with issues about the rationality of theory choice in science. The dissertation is much inspired by Hempel's work on explanation and scientific theories. Later on, Nozick would return to some of these themes in his book *The Nature of Rationality.*

From 1963 to 1965, Nozick taught at Princeton as an assistant professor. He then moved to Harvard where he stayed for two years, followed by two years of teaching as an associate professor at Rockefeller University from 1967 to 1969. After his short stay at Rockefeller, Nozick returned to Harvard to become a full professor in 1969, at the age of 30, where he remained for the rest of his life. He was the chair of the Philosophy Department from 1981 to 1984. In 1985 he was awarded the Arthur Kingsley Porter Professorship of Philosophy and in 1998 he was named Joseph Pellegrino University Professor.

Nozick acquired fame through the publication of his masterpiece *Anarchy, State, and Utopia* in 1974. In this book, Nozick advances his libertarian political and moral theory. Together with John Rawls's *A Theory of Justice,* it constitutes a keystone of twentieth-century political philosophy that was crucial to the revival of the discipline. His work made libertarianism respectable and helped to set the agenda for political theory up to the present day. It has generated much discussion and has been taken seriously by a broad range of thinkers.

Early on Nozick was a committed socialist. At school, he joined Norman Thomas's Socialist Party. While an undergraduate at Columbia, he founded the local chapter of the Student League for Industrial Democracy (which would later change its name to Students for a Democratic Society). Growing up, he had simply taken socialism for granted and was never confronted with well-worked out arguments in favour of capitalism. It was only after starting graduate studies at Princeton that he was introduced to pro-capitalist ideas. In particular, arguments with his friend Bruce Goldberg had familiarized him with libertarian theory. An important catalyst in his shift towards libertarian political philosophy was a conversation with Murray Rothbard around 1968 (cf. p. xv). Goldberg invited him along to a meeting of the Circle Bastiat, where Nozick's discussion with Rothbard made him realize the strength of libertarianism and the importance of the anarchist's challenge to the idea that states can be legitimate.

Initially, he wanted to refute libertarian views. Yet, ultimately he was convinced by the arguments, becoming a libertarian with reluctance. Many of the considerations and arguments that led to this change are presented in *Anarchy, State, and Utopia*. The book was mostly written while Nozick was a fellow at the Center for the Advanced Study in Behavioral Sciences at Palo Alto in 1971–1972. While in Stanford, he intended to work on the problem of free will and he describes *Anarchy, State, and Utopia* as 'an accident' (Nozick: 1997, p. 1).

Part I of *Anarchy, State, and Utopia* arose out of a talk given to a Stanford student group in which Nozick presented some thoughts on how a state would arise out of the state of nature. The first part tries to take up the anarchist's challenge by showing that it is possible for a state to arise in a legitimate way. Part II is the result of a series of lectures given at Harvard as part of a course entitled 'Capitalism and Socialism' that Nozick co-taught with Michael Walzer. In this part, Nozick develops his entitlement theory of justice and criticizes his colleague John Rawls, responding to his book *A Theory of Justice* which was published in 1971. Nozick tries to draw the boundaries of legitimate state action, by arguing that considerations regarding justice do not warrant any extension of the state beyond the minimal state. Part III is based on an essay on utopia that was presented at a meeting of the American Philosophical Association. In this part, Nozick sketches a libertarian utopia, whereby the utopia amounts to a framework for utopia, that is, a framework in which people can pursue their own utopias.

Anarchy, State, and Utopia was awarded the National Book Award in 1975 and is widely acclaimed as one of the most important contributions to political philosophy in the twentieth century. The Times Literary Supplement named it as one of 'The Hundred Most Influential Books Since the War'. Nozick's theories have been subjected to much criticism and a huge amount of secondary literature has been generated. Nozick never responded to any of the criticisms on the basis that he 'did not want to spend my life writing "The Son of Anarchy, State, and Utopia," "The Return of the Son of . . .," etc. I had other philosophical questions to think about' (Nozick: 1997, p. 2).

These other questions were concerned with more abstract philosophical issues, which he discusses in his book *Philosophical Explanations*, published in 1981. This book was Nozick's next big project. It was awarded the Ralph Waldo Emerson Award of Phi Beta Kappa. Again, Nozick managed to produce a wide-ranging and fascinating book that has had an important impact on the philosophical landscape. In particular, his truth-tracking theory of knowledge and his closest-continuer account of personal identity have created large secondary literatures and have been reprinted in many anthologies and collections.

Philosophical Explanations is divided into three main sections: Metaphysics, Epistemology and Value. In the Introduction, Nozick sets out his characteristic philosophical methodology. For him, philosophy should not primarily be concerned with arguments that are aimed at proving a particular thesis. Philosophers should not focus on convincing opponents of the theory, but rather be concerned with the exploration of conceptual connections, as well as with explanations of how things can be possible. In Part I, Nozick tackles some of the fundamental problems of metaphysics, including the question why there is something rather than nothing. He also proposes his influential closest-continuer approach for dealing with problems of personal identity. In Part II, he is concerned with epistemology and puts forward his famous truth-tracking account of knowledge and his discussion of scepticism. Part III is based on the theme of value, which includes discussions of free will, the foundations of ethics and the meaning of life.

The Examined Life was published in 1989. This is an accessible, popular, non-technical and wide-ranging book that is concerned with the meaning of life. Nozick discusses a broad range of issues, such as politics, happiness, love, reality, democracy and meaning. As we will see later on, in this book Nozick distances himself from the extreme form of libertarianism that he had espoused in *Anarchy, State, and Utopia.*

His next book, *The Nature of Rationality*, was published in 1993. It incorporates his Tanner Lectures on Human Values, entitled 'Decisions of Principle, Principles of Decision', that Nozick gave at Princeton University in 1991. It is a technical work that focuses on rational choice theory, decision theory and game theory. In this book, Nozick provides the canonical form of Newcomb's Problem which he had already discussed in his Ph.D. dissertation and which had a significant influence on decision theory. It also includes an important discussion of symbolic value that influenced his approach to political philosophy. It was as a result of thinking about decision theory that Nozick would come to appreciate the symbolic value of certain political actions, such as outlawing voluntary slavery, which then served to moderate his libertarianism.

In 1997 a collection of essays was published under the title *Socratic Puzzles*. These essays cover a broad range of topics, including discussions of coercion, Austrian methodology, moral structures, Newcomb's Problem, animal rights, as well as philosophical fiction.

In the spring of 1997 he delivered the prestigious John Locke lectures at Oxford University. The title of his lecture series was 'Invariance and Objectivity'. This was later to become the core of his final book *Invariances: The Structure of the Objective World*, which was published in 2001. This is a technical and specialized book that deals with questions about objectivity and truth. More precisely, Nozick provides a discussion of relativism about truth, an account of objectivity as invariance under various transformations, a sceptical discussion of necessary truths, as well as an evolutionary account of consciousness and ethics. The book includes a number of discussions of recent scientific theories and discoveries, in particular of quantum mechanics. A reviewer in *The Economist* nicely described the experience of reading this book as feeling 'like a social chess player accompanying a grandmaster down the tables at a simultaneous display, struggling to follow each game while listening to him explain how chess would work in six dimensions'.

During his career, Nozick received many academic honours. He was a fellow of the American Academy of Arts and Sciences, a member of the Council of Scholars of the Library of Congress, a corresponding fellow of the British Academy and a senior fellow of the Society of Fellows at

Harvard. He was president of the American Philosophical Association's Eastern Division and in 1998 he received the Presidential Citation from the American Psychological Association. He held fellowships from the Guggenheim Foundation, the Rockefeller Foundation, the National Endowment for the Humanities, and the Center for Advanced Study in the Behavioral Sciences.

Robert Nozick died on 23 January 2002 at the age of 63 as a result of stomach cancer that had been diagnosed in 1994.

Nozick's approach to philosophy

Nozick had a very distinctive approach to philosophy that is reflected in his manner of argumentation, in his style of writing, in the scope of subjects he discussed as well as in the range of sources he drew on. He described his style of argumentation as 'philosophical exploration' (p. xii), seeing himself as being engaged in an open-ended inquiry that does not purport to give any definitive answers. He does not present his views in a unified and monolithic system and sometimes it is not clear to what extent there is a larger system, rather than there merely being a collection of reflections and explorations. His primary concern is to explore the conceptual landscape, to try out new things, raise doubts, suggest solutions and identify connections. As a result of raising new problems and identifying novel avenues of inquiry, he often leaves the reader with more questions than answers. This approach is nicely summed up in his famous quote that '[t]here is room for words on subjects other than last words' (p. xii).

While his early work fits squarely into mainstream analytic philosophy, he became somewhat critical of certain features of this philosophical approach. Already in *Anarchy, State, and Utopia* we find a critical description of analytic philosophy (p. x). He slowly drifted away from an emphasis on arguments that try to convince an opponent to exploring issues, opening up possibilities and trying to uncover interesting conceptual connections. Nozick describes his approach as non-coercive philosophy that attempts to explain rather than convince and that aims at understanding rather than proof. This differentiation from analytic philosophy becomes more marked in some of his later works, in particular in less technical work such as *The Examined Life*.

His inventive and explorative approach to philosophy is reflected in his style of writing. Though often technical, his works are always enjoyable to read. His writing is very lively and does not amount to a rigid exposition of a philosophical system. He is particularly skilful in finding memorable and convincing examples and thought experiments. The Wilt Chamberlain example and the 'experience machine' thought experiment are two cases in point, which we will be discussing later on. He was also adept in finding expressions that manage to convey a great deal of meaning and get integrated into standard philosophical discourse, such as his notion of 'truth-tracking' in epistemology.

While being inventive, witty and playful, his argumentation is at the same time highly sophisticated and often makes use of technical and formal tools. For example, in *Anarchy, State, and Utopia* he avails himself of decision theory, game theory and economic theory, appealing in particular to evolutionary accounts and invisible-hand explanations. Nozick adopts a very ecumenical approach, drawing on a wide array of different sources and utilizing various techniques and formal methods developed in different disciplines. He takes insights and inspiration from subjects ranging from Buddhism to evolutionary biology, from literature to quantum mechanics, from economics to sociology.

Nozick had wide-ranging interests and published on a diverse set of topics. He is a fascinating, deep and original thinker, who engaged with a broad range of subjects, always finding interesting and insightful ways of approaching philosophical problems, while drawing on many different sources. Though he is often classified as a political philosopher, this is a label that he himself rejected since most of his work was concerned with other issues. He covered an extensive range of topics both in research and in teaching. He taught a wide variety of courses, including courses on capitalism, the Russian revolution, evolutionary biology and the meaning of life and only once in his life did Nozick teach the same course twice.

2

Critical Exposition

Famously, Nozick begins his book *Anarchy, State, and Utopia* with the claim: 'Individuals have rights, and there are things no person or group may do to them (without violating their rights)' (p. ix). This claim constitutes the basis of Nozick's political philosophy and moral outlook. His book is an attempt to examine the implications of this claim for our understanding of the legitimate functions of the state, while also providing support in favour of this moral outlook and criticisms of alternative views. He intends to assess whether the existence of a state can be justified at all and what functions it can legitimately perform. In particular, he takes the anarchist's challenge seriously and raises the question whether the acceptance of individual rights leaves any room for legitimate governments. He argues against the anarchist's claim that every form of government is illegitimate, that states are intrinsically immoral and that only anarchy constitutes a justified societal arrangement. Having defended the legitimacy of the state, he then challenges the dominant view by showing that only a minimal state is legitimate and that anything more extensive violates rights.

Nozick summarizes the main conclusions of his book by saying that 'a minimal state, limited to the narrow functions of protection against force, theft, fraud, enforcement of contracts, and so on, is justified; that any more extensive state will violate persons' rights not to be forced to do certain things, and is unjustified; and that the minimal state is inspiring as well as right' (p. ix). That is, the state is not intrinsically immoral, but can arise in a legitimate manner. In other words, the anarchist's challenge can be met insofar as we can find room for a legitimate state that is compatible with individual rights. (This is what Nozick attempts to establish in Part I.) Nonetheless, rights place important constraints on any legitimate state, thereby ensuring that only a minimal state is justified. If a state transgresses the narrow boundaries defined by rights, then it becomes an illegitimate state since it violates the rights of individuals. (This is the conclusion of Part II.) Moreover, Nozick contends, a minimal state that complies with these moral restrictions constitutes an attractive ideal since it is a framework for utopia. Not only is a minimal state the only legitimate state, it is also an inspiring state. (This is argued for in Part III.)

This is a radical political philosophy that has many important implications. For example, it implies that the state is not permitted to coerce people to help others and is not allowed to coerce people for their own good. Neither altruistically nor paternalistically inspired intervention is justified. The welfare of other people or of oneself does not constitute an adequate ground for justifying interference. Rights are side constraints on actions and trump all competing considerations, such as considerations of equality or welfare. Redistributionist policies are consequently ruled out as illegitimate. The same holds for various regulations attempting to modify the behaviour of individuals by rendering actions that are deemed to be undesirable either more expensive or even outright illegal. Such prohibitions, regulations and paternalistic policies are ruled out by the rights of individuals. In short, there is no room for redistribution or paternalism within a Nozickian state.

This criticism and rejection of coercion and force is combined with an emphasis on voluntarism that is present throughout Nozick's works. He wants to minimize the use of force and coercion, restricting its legitimate employment to the protection of individual rights. Governments, as well as individuals, are not permitted to restrain or constrain others for altruistic or paternalistic reasons. This does not, however, imply that non-coercive strategies for the achievement of these goals are ruled out. On the contrary, they can be praiseworthy and we might have non-enforceable duties to engage in them. The only thing that is problematic is the attempt to achieve these goals by coercive means, in particular by means of the coercive apparatus of the state.

Nozick does not deny that we have obligations to help others. He only denies that these obligations are enforceable, that we can be coerced to fulfil them and that it is the role of the state to achieve these goals. 'In no way does political philosophy or the realm of the state exhaust the realm of the morally desirable or moral oughts. . . . [R]ights are not the whole of what we want a society to be like, or of how we morally ought to behave toward one another' (Nozick: 1981, p. 503). Accordingly, it is important to keep in mind that Nozick is restricting his focus in *Anarchy, State, and Utopia* to those obligations that are enforceable since they are the proper subject matter of political philosophy.

Thus, we can capture the key features of his political philosophy, by noting that it is (i) a theory based on individual rights, that (ii) allows that a minimal state is justified, while (iii) restricting state action such that nothing more than a minimal state can be legitimate, claiming that (iv) such a state is inspiring and right. These are the four key aspects of Nozick's political philosophy. The present chapter will follow this progression, beginning with an outline of the moral theory that Nozick adopts, followed by his response to the anarchist's challenge. We will then look at the limits of the state that Nozick identifies, which restrict legitimate state actions to those of a minimal state, before assessing his view that such a minimal state is an inspiring ideal. The chapter concludes with a brief analysis of the evolution of Nozick's thought after the publication of *Anarchy, State, and Utopia.*

Accordingly, our discussion in this chapter will more-or-less follow the mode of presentation that Nozick makes use of in *Anarchy, State, and Utopia.* The only difference being that instead of dividing the discussion into three parts, we divide it into five by adding a separate discussion of Nozick's moral philosophy, as well as a description of his thought post-*Anarchy, State, and Utopia.* The reason for the former alteration is that Nozick does not provide a unified and systematic account of morality. Instead, his discussion of such issues is spread throughout *Anarchy, State, and Utopia* as well as some of his other writings. It will be useful to try to synthesize these various statements since a systematic account of Nozick's ethical thought will be important for evaluating and understanding the rest of his project.

A few methodological disclaimers are in order. Due to considerations of space, we will only focus on Nozick's main line of argumentation in favour of the minimal state and against any more extensive state. This requires us to leave aside many of Nozick's insightful and fascinating tangential discussions and intellectual excursions, such as his treatment of animal rights, his discussion of the Marxist theory of exploitation, and his account of demoktesis ('ownership of the people, by the people and for the people', cf. p. 290). Similarly, we will not consider in detail Nozick's lengthy critique of Rawls's *A Theory of Justice* as well as other sometimes technical discussions, but only integrate them into the systematic exposition of Nozick's positive contribution when relevant. Moreover, Nozick's discussions of ethics and politics in his other writings will be largely ignored, except when pertinent to the issues discussed in *Anarchy, State, and Utopia.*

The moral foundation

For Nozick political philosophy is applied moral philosophy. Moral philosophy provides the constraints within which a political theory can be formulated and the principles from which such a theory emerges. 'Moral philosophy sets the background for, and boundaries of, political philosophy. What persons may and may not do to one another limits what they may do through the apparatus of a state, or do to establish such an apparatus' (p. 6). Moreover, morality does not only set the limits of politics, but only by reference to moral considerations can the state be justified. 'The moral prohibitions it is permissible to enforce are the source of whatever legitimacy the state's fundamental coercive power has' (p. 6). The moral legitimacy of the state, if it has any, derives from the enforcement of moral prohibitions. The state can only be morally justified insofar as it enforces certain moral requirements.

Moral philosophy forms the foundation upon which political philosophy is built. Hence, in order to gain a proper understanding of Nozick's political theory, we must have a good grasp of his moral philosophy. Accordingly, we need to be clear about Nozick's views as to what moral prohibitions there are, what limits are placed on individuals by morality, what the status of them is and where they come from. These issues will be addressed in the first part of this chapter, where we will provide an outline of the moral theory that is presented in *Anarchy, State, and Utopia*, supplemented by arguments and considerations that Nozick develops in other works when these are of relevance.

Rights considered as side constraints

The defining feature of Nozick's moral philosophy, which is already revealed in the opening line of *Anarchy, State, and Utopia*, is that he advances a theory of individual rights. Within his moral theory, rights occupy a fundamental position and are considered as side constraints. By adopting this view of rights, Nozick distinguishes himself from (i) theories that do not appeal to rights, (ii) theories that, though appealing to rights, only accord rights a derivative position, and (iii) theories that, though including rights in a non-derivative manner, do not consider rights as side constraints, but rather include them in the moral goals. That is, Nozick is dealing with a rights-based theory of morality, according to which rights are non-derivative and have the status of absolute side constraints. These side constraints impose limits on what can legitimately be done. Certain actions or kinds of actions are ruled out as impermissible since they conflict with the rights of individuals.

The idea that rights are side constraints is central to Nozick's project. He distinguishes two ways in which a moral theory can integrate certain considerations, namely as moral constraints or as moral goals. The notions of moral goals and moral side constraints pertain to the form or structure of a moral theory. On the one hand, a theory can include a feature in the moral goal that is to be achieved. The feature is treated as an end and the theory tells us to act in such a way that the end is realized in an optimal manner. Here we have a goal-directed structure, whereby an end is identified that is to be achieved. On the other hand, a theory can integrate a feature as a moral constraint. The theory tells us to act in such a way that the constraints are not violated. Here we are dealing with a constraint-based structure, whereby constraints are specified that need to be respected.

Side constraints integrate a feature into a moral theory without including it as a goal or end that is to be achieved, but rather as a constraint upon actions. The moral constraints are not part of the goals that our actions should accomplish. Instead, these constraints limit how goals are to be achieved. Side constraints do not tell us what goals we should pursue, but only tell us which actions are permissible in the pursuit of our goals, whatever these goals may be. They rule out certain possible courses of action as impermissible, rather than positively prescribing which actions are to be performed. In other words, side constraints are not concerned with the ends that are to be achieved, but rather with the means that one is permitted to use in the achievement of ends.

Nozick argues that accounts of morality that are purely goal-directed and do not include any side constraints are problematic since they do not respect the inviolability of persons. It is in the nature of purely goal-directed theories that there will be cases in which they require us to sacrifice individuals to achieve the goals of the moral theory. They do not accord individuals an inviolable status but tell us to treat people as mere means if this is required for achieving the moral goal in an optimal manner. This is particularly clear, for example, in the case of utilitarianism. Utilitarianism is a theory that has a purely goal-directed structure, whereby utility is identified as the moral goal which ought to be maximized. We can easily imagine cases where the maximization of utility requires sacrificing the well-being and possibly even the life of an individual for the sake of maximizing overall utility. Nozick here mentions the well-known example that utilitarianism might require an innocent person to be punished to stop a mob from going on a vengeful rampage (cf. p. 28).

In order to avoid such unpalatable consequences, we need to include rights into our moral theory. Rights carve out a protected sphere around individuals, thereby making individuals inviolable. They reflect moral boundaries that are not to be transgressed. Including rights into a moral theory ensures that individuals ought not to be treated as mere means. Nozick argues that respecting the inviolability of persons requires us to accept a rights-based moral theory that treats rights as moral constraints.

Here it might be objected that if we care about rights, then we should try to minimize the violation of rights and accordingly include rights into the moral goal. Since rights are important, they should feature in the goals of the moral theory, rather than being treated as moral side constraints. The goals should specify that rights are to be respected and that rights violations are to be minimized. Put differently, the objection states that it is not the case that purely goal-directed theories per se fail to respect the inviolability of persons, but only unsophisticated ones that do not include rights in the moral goals.

Nozick rejects this suggestion and claims that it is not adequate to integrate rights into the moral goals. He argues that while rights are necessary for giving a satisfactory account that is not subject to these problems, the inclusion of rights is not sufficient. Even granting rights a non-derivative status is not sufficient. To avoid these problems rights have to be included in the correct manner, namely insofar as they are treated as side constraints. We can account for the inviolability of persons only if we consider rights as moral constraints on actions, rather than including rights in the moral goals that are specified by the theory.

The problem with goal-directed rights-based theories is that they do not succeed in capturing the inviolability of persons. The reason for including rights into our moral theory in the first place was to recognize certain moral boundaries between individuals, the violation of which is deemed unacceptable. The problem was that purely goal-directed moral theories, such as utilitarianism, classified certain actions that involved treating people as mere means as being permissible or even required. Accordingly, rights are included into the theory to capture the inviolability of persons. However, including rights into the moral goals and arguing that rights violations ought to be minimized does not in fact allow us to avoid this problem and does not capture the inviolability of persons. Indeed, this view is subject to the very same problems that it was intended to solve.

Rather than having a case where the minimization of disutility requires us to violate certain moral boundaries and treat an individual as a mere means in our pursuit of the moral goal, we now end up in a situation where the minimization of rights violations requires us to violate certain moral boundaries and treat an individual as a mere means towards achieving this moral goal. In such cases, rights violations can be justified in terms of the prevention of other rights violations. For instance, 'someone might try to justify his punishing another *he* knows to be innocent of a crime that enraged a mob, on the grounds that punishing this innocent person would help to avoid even greater violations of rights by others, and so would lead to a minimum weighted score for rights violations in the society' (p. 29).

If rights are included into the moral goal, then rights violations can be weighed up against each other, even if rights are granted a fundamental status. In Nozick's term, we end up with a 'utilitarianism of rights' (p. 28) that suffers from the same problems that the appeal to rights was supposed to solve. Thus we can see that the same problems reoccur at the level of rights and this holds independently of whether rights are given a derivative or a fundamental status. No matter how rights are understood, the moral theory will not account for the inviolability of persons as long as rights are included into the moral goals. This utilitarianism of rights does not adequately respect the moral status of individuals and does not capture the moral boundaries separating different persons.

The problem of not being able to respect the inviolability of persons is a structural problem pertaining to purely goal-directed theories per se that cannot be solved by specifying particular goals or modifying our understanding of the goals. The conclusion is that purely goal-directed moral theories cannot capture the inviolability of persons. The reasons for rejecting simple goal-directed accounts, such as utilitarianism, are reasons for rejecting purely goal-directed moral theories per se. A different kind of moral theory is required in order to make room for the inviolability of persons. To do so, we need to include moral constraints into our theory, rather than only specifying the goals that are to be achieved. It is not enough to have a rights-based theory. It is not even enough to have rights-based theory whereby rights are granted a fundamental status. To get a moral theory that respects the inviolability of persons, rights have to be treated as side constraints.

What we need are side constraints since these impose moral restrictions the transgression of which cannot be justified in terms of the prevention of other transgressions. Side constraints rule out a utilitarianism of rights since they are not concerned with maximizing rights compliance, but instead place restrictions upon permissible actions. Rights are not included as part of the moral goals, as happens in utilitarianism, but rather constrain the achievement of goals. Only if we have such side constraints do we have a moral theory that places an absolute restriction upon treating people as mere means.

It should be noted that whether side constraints really are absolute in a strict sense is a problem that Nozick sidesteps. 'The question of whether these side constraints are absolute, or whether they may be violated in order to avoid catastrophic moral horror, and if the latter, what the resulting structure might look like, is one I hope largely to avoid' (p. 30, footnote). While it is clear that a moral theory should include rights, and while it is clear that side constraints are superior to other conceptions that allow for a utilitarianism of rights, it is nonetheless difficult to bite the bullet and claim that side constraints may never legitimately be infringed upon. Those who allow for exceptions in cases of catastrophes manage to avoid the counter-intuitive consequences that follow from an absolutist conception of side constraints. However, they face the daunting task of giving a principled account of side constraints that is not ad hoc and that makes them neither absolute nor subject to maximization (cf. Nozick: 1981, p. 495).

The basis of libertarian side constraints

Nozick argues that rights are side constraints that reflect the inviolability of persons. These side constraints embody the libertarian prohibition on aggression, ruling out redistribution and paternalism as being morally impermissible. Individual rights prohibit the use of force and the threat of force except in cases of self-defence. We have seen Nozick's arguments to the effect that we need to include rights into our moral theory as side constraints if we are to respect the inviolability of persons and avoid cases in which people are treated as mere means in the achievement of a moral goal. It is now time to turn to the question of why we should accept the inviolability of persons and why the side constraints following therefrom should turn out to be libertarian side constraints. That is, on the one hand, the question arises as to what it is that gives rise to moral constraints, what counts as the basis of rights and why we should consider persons as inviolable. On the other hand, there is the question why the required side constraints are the libertarian side constraints that rule out redistribution and paternalism.

To begin with, it is important to note that Nozick is not engaged in a foundational project whereby individual rights are deduced from a set of self-evident axioms. He does not start from ground zero to build up a moral theory. Instead, he puts forward an intuitively appealing position and attempts to work out its consequences, showing that it leads to a coherent and attractive account of political philosophy, while also providing criticisms of the available alternatives. Nonetheless, he does provide us with

some insight into the source and basis of rights. In particular, he considers a Kantian grounding for rights. 'Side
constraints upon action reflect the underlying Kantian
principle that individuals are ends and not merely means;
they may not be sacrificed or used for the achieving of
other ends without their consent. Individuals are inviolable'
(pp. 30–31).

The Kantian principle tells us to treat individuals as ends,
rather than merely treating them as means. This requires
us to treat them as beings that have dignity, beings that
freely choose how to act and that can set ends for themselves. In other words, treating them as ends requires us to
respect their freedom, to respect their choices, to respect
the ends that they have set for themselves. They are not
merely to be considered as means or tools that can be used
for the achievement of our ends, but as beings that have
their own ends that they themselves have chosen. Individuals should not be coerced since coercion amounts to
treating them as mere means. Coercion involves making
people do things that they have not chosen to do. It makes
them into means for the achievement of these ends. They
are used as tools for achieving ends that are alien to them.
They are coerced into doing things that they have not set
as ends for themselves. To treat individuals as ends, on the
contrary, amounts to respecting the ends that they have set
for themselves, to respecting their choices and not inter-
fering with their freedom. We should let others pursue
their ends in the way they see fit, rather than manipulating
them for our own ends or imposing ends upon them that
they have not chosen for themselves.

Since individuals ought to be treated as ends and not as
mere means, it follows that they should not be coerced to
do things against their will. Individuals themselves determine their lives and no one can legitimately force them to

live in a particular way. We cannot legitimately impose ends upon them. This means that paternalistic interventions are prohibited. People ought to be free to lead their lives the way they want (as long as they do not violate the rights of someone else). We cannot tell them how to live. We can only suggest to them how they should live. We can try to convince them to act in certain ways. However, in the end, they always have to set their own ends and freely accept or reject our suggestions and recommendations. Thus, the fact that individuals are ends and not mere means gives rise to the libertarian prohibition on paternalistic interferences. Coercion is ruled out and the freedom of individuals has to be respected. Side constraints reflect the fact that we have to respect that different people have their own projects to pursue, that they have to set their own ends and lead their lives the way they see fit.

Thus, in order to respect the inviolability of persons, we have to treat individuals as ends and not as mere means. Doing so requires us to not violate their rights, to not interfere with their choices, but to let them freely decide which ends to pursue and how to live their lives. The question now arises why persons are inviolable in this sense, what it is that makes it necessary that they be treated as ends. Nozick approaches this question by considering some of the traditional answers that have been given, such as the claim that individuals are rational, possess free will or are moral agents. He is not satisfied with any of these answers. Each trait considered on its own seems insufficient to give rise to moral constraints. Just because someone is rational or because someone possesses free will does not mean that that person ought not to be treated in certain ways. Instead of opting for one of these traditional answers, he suggests that we should consider them collectively and add as an additional feature the ability to shape one's life in accordance with some overall conception that one has chosen. The reason why this collection of capacities and characteristics matters and gives rise to moral constraints, Nozick conjectures, 'is connected with that elusive and difficult notion: the meaning of life. A person's shaping his life in accordance with some overall plan is his way of giving meaning to his life; only a being with the capacity to so shape his life can have or strive for meaningful life' (p. 50).

Hence, persons are beings who can shape their lives according to a conception or plan that they themselves have framed. They thereby possess the capacity to impart meaning to their lives and it is because of this that they are inviolable, that they should be treated as ends and not as mere means. By respecting their rights, we respect and adequately respond to the fact that people have the capacity to shape their lives and strive for meaning. As he puts it in one of his later works, recognizing 'a domain of autonomy constitutes responsiveness to a value-seeking self' (Nozick: 1981, p. 503). This line of argument requires an account of what matters in life and what makes life meaningful. Nozick discusses these issues at length in some of his other writings, in particular in *Philosophical Explanations* and in *The Examined Life.* In *Anarchy, State, and Utopia,* we find some indication as to why the voluntary adopting of ends is so important, why it matters that people freely set ends for themselves and actively pursue them as they see fit.

Nozick argues that what gives meaning to life is more than just the experiences had by the individual. A meaningful life is spent not just as a passive recipient of experiences, but as an active agent who can shape his life according to the plans that he has adopted. This emphasis on leading one's life is supported by Nozick's thought experiment involving an 'experience machine'. Nozick devises a thought experiment that is intended to discredit the claim made by utilitarians that all that matters are experiences. He asks us to consider a scenario in which we have the option of plugging into machines that can make us have any experiences whatsoever. The question then arises whether we should plug into such a machine. The utilitarian will be committed to the claim that we should plug in. This is because these machines allow us to maximize pleasurable experiences and this is all that matters for the utilitarian.

Nozick, however, wants to say that there is something wrong about plugging into such a machine, that there is more to a worthwhile and meaningful life than being a subject of pleasurable experiences. In particular, being plugged into such a machine undermines our status of being active agents who lead their own lives. As Nozick notes: 'What is most disturbing about them [i.e. experience machines] is their living of our lives for us' (p. 44). In other words, the thought experiment brings out the importance of activity and achievement. A person is not just a passive locus of utility, a subject of experiences. Instead, a person is an autonomous being who decides how to live his or her life, who sets and pursues ends. The importance of leading a life, of pursuing projects that one has chosen and of achieving goals that one has set for oneself is left out by utilitarian accounts. Utilitarianism is thus problematic in that it treats individuals merely as (passive) loci of utility. Instead, we should take account of the importance of autonomous agency and of leading and shaping one's life since these features are crucial aspects of a meaningful life. Violating the rights of individuals and failing to treat them as ends amounts to undercutting their ability to impart meaning to their lives and to treating them as mere things or tools the lives of which do not have any meaning and real significance of their own.

Nozick supplements these Kantian considerations, by appealing to the separateness of persons. Not only do we have to respect that individuals have their own lives to lead and their own ends to set, we also have to respect the separateness of persons and take seriously the moral boundaries that separate persons. That is, in addition to respecting the importance of leading one's own life and of setting ends for oneself, we have to respect that different people are separate and have different and separate lives to live. This means for Nozick that one should recognize that there is no social entity to which one can appeal in order to justify the sacrifice of an individual's good. 'There are only individual people, different individual people, with their own individual lives. Using one of these people for the benefit of others, uses him and benefits the others. Nothing more. What happens is that something is done to him for the sake of others. Talk of an overall social good covers this up' (p. 33).

The separateness of persons ensures that the Kantian principle not only rules out paternalism but also gives rise to the libertarian side constraint against redistribution, against sacrificing an individual for the sake of other people. In particular, Nozick appeals to the distinctness of individuals in order to criticize an argument in favour of forced redistribution. One may try to motivate redistribution by claiming that inter-personal redistribution is on a par with intra-personal redistribution. The defender of redistribution can try to argue that sacrificing one person's well-being for the greater social good is analogous to the unproblematic intra-personal case which consists in an individual sacrificing current pleasure for future happiness.

This argument, however, is undercut by the separateness of persons. Individuals are distinct and have separate lives to live. There is no 'social entity' and consequently 'no moral balancing act can take place among us' (p. 33). The bad that is done to one person is not cancelled out by the good done to another person in the way that the sacrifice of pleasure by my present self is cancelled out by the additional pleasure of my future self. There is a crucial difference between an inter-personal and an intra-personal redistribution. An intra-personal transfer, which is concerned with the case of earlier and later selves, seems entirely unproblematic. There is nothing wrong with making a present sacrifice for a future good. This situation is radically different from an inter-personal transfer, where something is taken from one person and given to another. In such a case, one person is made to sacrifice his or her well-being for that of another person, which is morally problematic since it involves treating that person as a mere means. There is no balancing of different people, no social entity of which the two are parts. This is unlike the person case, where an earlier and a later self are both parts of the same entity, namely a single person. The moral difference between these two cases thus derives from the fact that distinct persons are separate moral entities that are separated by moral boundaries. Hence, when combined with the separateness of persons, the Kantian idea that people should be treated as ends and not as mere means gives rise to moral boundaries that ought not to be transgressed. In particular, we can see that redistribution involves a transgression of a moral boundary and is therefore illegitimate.

Thus, we have seen that Nozick appeals to Kantian considerations about the inviolability of persons, as well as to the notion of the separateness of persons, to argue in favour of libertarian side constraints. The Kantian considerations

rule out paternalistic interventions since such interventions violate the autonomy of individuals and do not recognize that they have their own lives to lead, that they have
to set and pursue their own ends in order to impart meaning to their lives. When joined with the separateness of
persons and the denial of the existence of a social entity,
they also rule out redistributive interventions. This is
because the separateness of persons undermines the idea
that moral balancing acts can take place between persons
and that there are intersocietal sacrifices that are equally
unobjectionable as interpersonal sacrifices. Accordingly,
all cases of redistribution will be cases of treating some
people as mere means for bettering the situation of other
people. Thus, Nozick holds that individuals are inviolable
and have their own and separate lives to live and that neither
paternalistic nor redistributive interventions are morally
permissible.

Against anarchy

We have seen that Nozick's moral theory includes a strong
understanding of libertarian rights, which are considered
as moral side constraints on actions. Accepting such individual rights makes it questionable whether there can be a
legitimate state at all, whether the state can be justified.
Nozick takes the anarchist's challenge seriously and devotes
the first part of *Anarchy, State, and Utopia* to an attempt to
refute the anarchist.

State of nature theorizing

'The fundamental question of political philosophy, one
that precedes questions about how the state should be

organized, is whether there should be any state at all' (p. 4). Nozick thinks that we cannot simply take the legitimacy of the state for granted. Instead, the state has to be justified and the anarchist's challenge has to be met. This challenge is two-fold in nature. On the one hand, the anarchist claims that the state is intrinsically immoral. On the other, he argues that the state is a sub-optimal outcome and that we would be better off without a state. Nozick attempts to meet both of these challenges. The first challenge is met by showing that the state can arise without violating any rights. To show that states can arise in a legitimate way, i.e. in a way that does not involve rights violations, is not yet to provide positive justification for their existence. To fully justify the state we need to show not only that it is not intrinsically immoral but also that it is good. This is what Nozick tries to do. 'If one could show that the state would be superior even to this most favored situation of anarchy, the best that realistically can be hoped for, or would arise by a process involving no morally impermissible steps, or would be an improvement if it arose, this would provide a rationale for the state's existence; it would justify the state' (p. 5).

Roughly speaking, Nozick's strategy consists in giving an argument to the effect that a state would arise by means of an invisible-hand process without violating any rights. He argues that a state would arise out of a state of nature by means of a process that does not require any explicit intention to create a state. Instead, a state would be the spontaneous and unintended outcome of the actions of individuals in the state of nature. As he puts it, we would 'back into the state without really trying'.

It is important to note that Nozick is not interested in the justification of any existing state, but in 'explanatory political theory'. He attempts to provide a fundamental

explanation of the political realm, that is, an explanation
of the political realm in purely nonpolitical terms. An adequate theory of a state of nature that describes 'how a state
would arise from that state of nature will serve our explanatory purposes, *even if no actual state ever arose that way*' (p. 7).
This explanatory project partly accounts for why Nozick
provides an invisible-hand argument rather than a consent-
based justification of the state. It is not because he considers a state founded on explicit consent to be problematic.
Rather, it is because this would be a trivial case of a legitimate state that would not satisfy Nozick's explanatory purposes. A consent-based account, unlike an invisible-hand
argument, does not constitute a fundamental explanation.
It does not explain the political realm in non-political terms
since the state is the intended result of a social contract.
'Invisible-hand explanations of phenomena thus yield
greater understanding than do explanations of them as
brought about by design as the object of people's inten-
tions' (p. 19). Nozick does not just want to show that we
could consent to a state and thereby give rise to a legitimate state. Instead, he attempts to establish that we would
act in certain ways that give rise to a state, without anyone
intending to bring about a state.

Moreover, the absence of actual consent makes a consent-
based account largely irrelevant when it comes to assessing
existing states, while an invisible-hand approach allows for
relevance since the process is less distant from the actual
process. Nozick classifies an explanation as a 'potential
explanation' if it is one that does not fit the actual situation but would be the correct explanation if things were
different. Such an explanation shows how the state could
have arisen, but not how it actually did arise. The relevance
of a potential explanation decreases the more remote the

process that it invokes is from the actual process. Both consent-based accounts as well as Nozick's invisible-hand explanation are potential explanations. Yet, since the invisible-hand explanation is closer to the actual process than a consent-based explanation is, it is more relevant to what is actually going on (cf. pp. 293–294).

From anarchy to the minimal state

Nozick's discussion begins with the state of nature, with an anarchic situation in which individuals enforce their own rights. Nozick is willing to grant the anarchist a favourable description of the state of nature. He allows that there will be a general compliance with the dictates of morality. There will not be perfect compliance, but in most cases people will know what is right and will act accordingly. The cases when conflicts arise lead to what Locke called the inconveniences of the state of nature. These inconveniences primarily have to do with the administration of justice. Individuals will be biased when they judge their own case and there will be no impartial arbiter to settle disputes and provide backing for agreements. Moreover, individuals might lack the power to enforce their rights. Locke argued that we need to set up a state to deal with these problems.

Nozick, however, suggests that various private solutions can be devised to deal with these inconveniences. The state of nature has inconveniences, but it also has solutions to deal with them. In particular, people will join together to form mutual-protection associations. These will then evolve into professionalized protection agencies, due to the benefits of the division of labour and of specialization. Initially there will be several such associations or companies in a certain geographical region. However, after some time we will end up with a single dominant protective agency. The reason that Nozick provides in favour of this claim is that the value of being a client of a particular agency depends on the strength of that agency relative to other agencies, thereby making it rational for individuals to become clients of the strongest protection agency. 'Out of anarchy, pressed by spontaneous groupings, mutual-protection associations, division of labor, market pressures, economies of scale, and rational self-interest there arises something very much resembling a minimal state or a group of geographically distinct minimal states' (pp. 16–17).

Is the dominant agency a state? Nozick answers this question in the negative. A dominant protection agency fails to satisfy two conditions that are required for classifying as a state since (i) it does not claim a monopoly on the use of force and since (ii) it does not provide universal coverage but only protects its clients. More precisely, a private protection agency does not announce that it will punish everyone who uses force without express permission of the agency. Hence, it does not claim a monopoly on the use of force and thus does not constitute a state. Moreover, private agencies differ from states in that they only protect their members. It does not provide protection to everyone within its territory, but restricts its services to its clients who have paid for protection. In other words, the presence of independents who are not members of the dominant agency undermines both of these features since they enforce their own rights.

In order to become a state the dominant agency would have to claim a monopoly and prohibit independents from enforcing their rights. Additionally, it would have to provide them with protective services to ensure universal coverage which would involve charging its clients in order to provide this extra coverage. In this way the dominant agency would become a state. Yet, both steps seem morally problematic. On the one hand, the anarchist claims that the protective agency cannot legitimately prohibit independents from enforcing their rights. It does not seem to be morally permissible for an agency to claim or enforce a monopoly on the use of force. Claiming such a monopoly amounts to a violation of the rights of independents. On the other hand, taking resources from its clients to provide universal coverage seems to be an illegitimate form of redistribution that is in violation of a side constraint. Nozick, however, argues that both of these problems can be overcome and that a dominant agency can claim a monopoly and provide universal coverage without violating rights.

Nozick argues that independents can be prohibited from enforcing their rights since this kind of private enforcement is risky. Protective agencies have a duty to their customers to protect their procedural rights. They have to make sure that their clients are judged according to fair and reliable procedures. Given the uncertainty and risk involved in letting independents enforce their rights, Nozick claims that the protection of procedural rights requires prohibiting independents from enforcing their rights. 'Since the dominant protective association judges its own procedures to be both reliable and fair, and believes this to be generally known, it will not allow anyone to defend against *them*. . . . Although no monopoly is claimed, the dominant agency does occupy a unique position by virtue of its power' (p. 108). In this way we end up with a de facto monopoly. This is not a de jure monopoly since everyone has the same rights. It is not the case that the dominant agency has a special right that others lack. Instead, everyone has the same right of prohibiting others from using risky and unreliable methods. It simply happens to be the case that the dominant agency is in a position in which it is the only one who can make use of that right. We end up in a situation whereby the right of prohibiting the use of procedures deemed to be risky is such that the exercise of this right by the dominant agency prevents others from exercising it. This is because the right 'includes the right to stop others from wrongfully exercising the right, and only the dominant power will be able to exercise the right against all others' (p. 109).

Prohibiting independents from enforcing their rights, however, requires the agency to compensate the independents for not being allowed to exercise their rights, which can be done by providing them with protection services free of charge. 'The clients of the protective agency, then, must compensate the independents for the disadvantages imposed upon them by being prohibited self-help enforcement of their own rights against the agency's clients' (p. 110). Nozick emphasizes that the resulting state is not a redistributive state. While the agency charges its clients to pay for protecting independents, this is not a redistributive activity. In order to judge whether an activity is redistributive, we need to assess the rationale for the activity rather than only assessing whether resources are taken from some and given to others. Since the provision of services to independents paid for by clients is based on the principle of compensation rather than on a redistributive principle that aims to achieve a certain distributive pattern, it follows that the resulting minimal state is not a redistributive state.

Thus, we started with anarchy and ended up with a minimal state. Out of anarchy emerges a dominant protective agency. This agency will become an ultraminimal state since it will claim a de facto monopoly on the use of force, given that it is going to prohibit independents from enforcing their rights against its clients. The ultraminimal state then has to be transformed into a minimal state since it must compensate the independents for having prohibited them from enforcing their rights by giving them free coverage. This implies that the provision of protection services has universal coverage. In this way the two features that were lacking have been met and we end up with a minimal state that is not based on redistributive principles but on the principle of compensation.

Nothing more than the minimal state

In the preceding part, we saw that Nozick thinks that the anarchist's challenge can be met and that a state can come into existence without violating anyone's rights. While Nozick believes that states can be legitimate, he also strongly defends the view that their legitimate functions are very restricted and that a minimal state is the only state that is justified. In order to defend this view, he provides a critique of some alternative conceptions of the state which grant it a more extensive role. Many reasons have been proposed as to why a minimal state is supposedly insufficient. Nozick's primary target is the claim that a more extensive state is required to achieve distributive justice. According to this proposal, a state must do more than protect life, liberty and property, by ensuring that a just distribution of goods obtains.

To begin with, Nozick points out that the very notion of distributive justice fails to be neutral. This is because the notion of 'distribution' suggests the idea that the goods that people possess have somehow been distributed and that this distribution may not have been adequate, thereby implying a need for re-distribution. Nozick rejects this conception on the basis that there is no central distribution of goods. He notes that 'we are not in the position of children who have been given portions of pie by someone who now makes last minute adjustments to rectify careless cutting' (p. 149). No one is in charge of allocating all the resources and determining what different people get. Instead, the possessions of individuals are determined by the multitude of actions and interactions among different individuals. People have the possessions they do, not because they have been distributed or allocated to them, but because they have acquired them from other people. To rectify this bias, Nozick suggests the notion of a 'holding'. Rather than holdings being somehow distributed by some centralized mechanism, the set of holdings emerges out of the voluntary exchanges and interactions among individuals.

Theories of justice

The problem of justice is to find out under what conditions the holdings of particular people are in conformity with the demands of justice. Before criticizing alternative accounts, Nozick first proceeds to specify what he considers to be the correct theory of justice in holdings, which he labels the 'entitlement theory of justice'. This theory consists of three components, namely (i) principles of justice in acquisition, (ii) principles of justice in transfer and (iii) principles of justice in rectification. The first set of principles specifies the conditions under which unowned resources may be appropriated, that is, the conditions under which initial holdings may justly be acquired. The second set of principles characterizes how holdings can be justly transferred from one person to another or how a holding may appropriately be returned to the condition of being unowned. Finally, the third set of principles is concerned with the question of how past injustices can be rectified, specifying how violations of the previous two sets of principles are to be dealt with. These three sets of principles exhaust the account of justice and fully determine the conditions under which particular sets of holdings are just.

In setting out the entitlement theory, Nozick does not provide us with the particular principles of justice and does not engage in the difficult task of specifying the precise conditions of the various principles. Instead, he only sets out the formal structure of the entitlement theory, specifying what kinds of principles it requires. This is for the most part sufficient for his aims since he does not intend to give a fully worked out account of justice. Instead, he simply wants to characterize the structure of the entitlement conception in order to be able to distinguish it from the end-state and patterned conceptions of justice which he will criticize later on. In this way, he can undermine alternative conceptions of justice that require a more extensive state, while specifying the framework of his entitlement theory which is perfectly compatible with a minimal state (cf. pp. 202–203).

While not providing a detailed account of any of these principles, Nozick discusses the issue of appropriation at some length. The problem of appropriation is how unowned resources initially get appropriated, how a moral claim to an unowned object can arise. Nozick takes Locke's discussion of appropriation as a starting point. In the *Second Treatise* Locke argued that it is possible to acquire a property right in something that was previously unowned

by mixing one's labour with it. He argues that we own our-
selves as well as our labour and that by mixing something
that we own, namely our labour, with something that is
unowned, namely the object, we come to own the object.
This account faces numerous difficulties and Nozick raises
several objections to it that focus on why the mixing of
labour gives rise to ownership, on what the mixing of labour
consists in, and on how far the property rights extend. For
example, he asks why I get to own the whole thing with
which I mix my labour, rather than losing my labour or
only acquiring partial ownership in the object. Similarly, he
asks why enclosing a piece of land by building a fence gives
rise to a property right to the enclosed land, rather than
only to the land immediately underneath the fence.

Rather than trying to respond to these objections to
Locke's account, Nozick rejects the idea that appropriation requires the mixing of labour with unowned objects.
Unfortunately, Nozick does not specify any other condition
that could replace the one proposed by Locke. All that
we are told is that the principles of justice in acquisition
specify the procedures by means of which individuals
can acquire legitimate claims over unowned objects. What
exactly these procedures involve, however, is something
that Nozick does not tell us.

Whatever these procedures may turn out to be, the question will arise whether there are any limits on appropriation, whether there are any restrictions on what and
how much can be appropriated. In discussing this question, Nozick again takes Locke's theory as a starting point.
According to Locke, appropriation is only justified on
condition that it leaves enough and as good for others
to appropriate. Nozick thinks that this proviso is too
restrictive and that it ignores the fact that appropriation is
generally beneficial for everyone insofar as private property

rights give rise to incentive structures that ensure that overall welfare is increased. Accordingly, Nozick proposes his own proviso to the effect that an appropriation is justified on condition that it leaves no one worse off than they would have been had the resource remained unowned. That is, the private ownership of a resource must be sufficiently beneficial to ensure that those who are no longer at liberty to use the resource are not worsened by the appropriation. This condition should not be understood as a utilitarian justification of property but as a condition that ensures that others are not harmed by an appropriation (cf. p. 177).

The proviso not only affects original acquisition, but also casts a 'historical shadow' on the transfer of property (cf. pp. 179–181). The limits on acquiring holdings by original acquisition also constitute limits on acquiring holdings by voluntary exchange. In particular, transfers of holdings may not lead to a situation whereby anyone is worse off than he would have been had those holdings remained unowned. For instance, if the original appropriation of all the water holes in a desert is ruled out by the proviso, then the acquisition of all these water holes by transfer is equally ruled out by the historical shadow of the proviso. Accordingly, it turns out that being voluntary is not a sufficient condition for a transfer to be justice-preserving – it also has to satisfy the proviso. If the proviso is violated, then one of two things needs to happen. Either compensation is due to bring it about that the position of others is no longer worsened. Or there will be limits on how the owner may use his property, namely he may use it only in such a way that the position of others is not worsened. For instance, the owner may not exclude others from using the property or may only charge them a limited amount.

This proviso allows Nozick to avoid counter-intuitive consequences that would otherwise arise in cases in which someone appropriates all the supply of a vital resource. Without the proviso, we would end up in a situation whereby others would be completely dependent on the person possessing this resource. Nozick, however, can say that such appropriations are not problematic since the proviso ensures that the person may not use his property in any way that worsens the situation of others relative to the baseline situation in which they are at liberty to use these things. It is important to note that property rights are not overridden in such cases by considerations concerning the well-being of others. Instead, the proviso is internal to the theory of property, which means that rights are restricted by the proviso rather than being overridden. Put differently, this means that there are no considerations extraneous to the theory of property that could trump property rights (cf. p. 180). Nozick can accordingly still accept that property rights are absolute (possibly excepting cases of 'catastrophic moral horror') since the proviso operates on the content of these rights.

While Nozick's discussion of how property rights arise is rather sketchy, and while many questions and problems still have to be dealt with, he points out that alternative accounts are no better off. Everyone has to give a theory of property rights and provide an account as to how objects can be appropriated. Simply stating that property is not private but communal does not solve this problem. A theoretical justification and explanation of property rights still has to be given. It has to be explained how a moral right over objects arises and this has not been achieved by any of Nozick's opponents.

The principles of justice in transfer constitute the next component of the entitlement theory. They are intended to specify the conditions under which we can move from one just set of holdings to another set of holdings in a justice-preserving manner. This includes, on the one hand, a characterization of the processes of transferring holdings that are justified. For Nozick, these processes include voluntary exchanges as well as gifts. On the other hand, these principles describe the kinds of processes whereby a new set of holding arises in a manner that is in violation of justice. Such processes include fraud, theft and coerced transfers.

Again, Nozick does not discuss these processes and procedures in any detail. He does, however, respond to the common objection that many apparently voluntary exchanges fail to preserve justice since they do not really classify as being voluntary, given that one of the persons involved in the exchange only has a very limited set of options. For example, it is often claimed that a choice between starving to death and accepting to work for a low wage is not a real choice and that the acceptance of the contract is not a voluntary action. Nozick responds: 'Whether a person's actions are voluntary depends on what it is that limits his alternatives. . . . Other people's actions place limits on one's available opportunities. Whether this makes one's resulting action non-voluntary depends upon whether these others had the right to act as they did' (p. 262). This means that whether an action is voluntary does not depend on the range of options available to the agent, but instead upon how the choice situation arose. If everyone acted within their rights and someone ends up finding himself in an unpalatable choice situation, then that person is not coerced no matter how limited and unpleasant the available choices turn out to be. For a choice to be involuntary, the choice situation must have arisen in a way that violates the rights of the person making the choice.

Finally, Nozick provides a brief discussion of issues pertaining to the rectification of past injustices. He raises a
number of important issues, such as the question whether
'an injustice [can be] done to someone whose holding was
itself based upon an unrectified injustice' (p. 152) and the
question as to how far back one must go 'in wiping clean
the historical slate of injustices' (p. 152). However, he does
not provide any answers to these questions but only states
that an ideal theory of rectification would make use of
various subjunctive conditionals to ascertain what would
have happened had the injustices not occurred. The lack
of historical and subjunctive information, as well as the
absence of a worked out theory of rectification severely
restricts the applicability of the entitlement theory to real
world cases. Nozick notes that 'one *cannot* use the analysis
and theory presented here to condemn any particular
scheme of transfer payments, unless it is clear that no
considerations of rectification of injustice could apply to
justify it. Although to introduce socialism as the punish-
ment for our sins would be to go too far, past injustices
might be so great as to make necessary in the short run
a more extensive state in order to rectify them' (p. 231).

Thus, according to Nozick, justice in holdings is determined by the three sets of principles that determine justice in acquisition, transfer and rectification. Whether a
set of holdings is in conformity with justice depends upon
whether the way it arose was in conformity with these principles. A holding is just if and only if it has been arrived
at by actions conforming to the principles of justice. These
principles are justice-preserving, which means that if a set
of holdings is just, then any application of these principles
ensures that justice is preserved such that the outcome is
just as well. 'A distribution is just if it arises from another

just distribution by legitimate means' (p. 151). According to the entitlement theory, one cannot arrive at an unjust set of holdings from a just set of holdings if the former was arrived at from the latter only by just steps. An injustice must have occurred at some point in arriving at a particular set of holdings in order for that set of holdings to be unjust.

The entitlement theory is a historical conception of justice. This means that the justice of a set of holdings is determined by how it arose, by the historical processes from which it resulted. This conception is to be contrasted with time-slice or end-state principles of justice, which are studied in welfare economics. These kinds of principles are not concerned with the historical genesis of a particular distribution, but only with its structural characteristics. They characterize justice in terms of how the holdings are distributed at a time or over an interval of time. In other words, they are merely concerned with the question of who ends up with which holdings. As a result, these accounts do not make room for particular entitlements to particular holdings, but treat structurally identical distributions as being equally just. They are thereby distinctly ahistorical. This is problematic since we often consider it relevant how a set of holdings arose, for example when we distinguish the situation in which a person has acquired an object as a gift from the situation in which he has acquired it by theft. The situations are identical as regards the distribution of goods insofar as the same person ends up with the same object. Yet, while the former situation is unproblematic, the latter is to be condemned. The difference between these situations that explains this moral difference is to be located in the historical processes that gave rise to them. While gift-giving is justice-preserving, theft is not a legitimate principle of transfer. Accordingly, we can see that whether people are entitled to something depends on how they got it. 'In contrast to end-result principles of justice, *historical principles* of justice hold that past circumstances or actions of people can create differential entitlements or differential deserts to things' (p. 155).

While the entitlement theory is a historical conception of justice and as such needs to be distinguished from end-state principles of justice, we must also distinguish it from other historical accounts. In particular, the entitlement theory has to be differentiated from patterned conceptions of justice. These conceptions specify some natural dimension or set of dimensions along which sets of holdings are supposed to be patterned. 'Let us call a principle of distribution *patterned* if it specifies that a distribution is to vary along some natural dimension, weighted sum of natural dimensions, or lexicographic ordering of natural dimensions' (p. 156). Well-known examples of patterned accounts include the principles that holdings should be distributed in accordance with need, merit or marginal contribution. It should be noted that even though many patterned principles have historical elements, some turn out to be ahistorical, for example the principle to distribute in accordance with IQ.

Though Nozick is not particularly clear about the relations between the different accounts of justice, we can see that there is a fundamental distinction between structural and procedural conceptions of justice. Structural theories can be distinguished into different kinds depending on whether the structuring principle is supplied by some independent dimension or variable in accordance with which holdings should be structured or whether the structuring principle is only concerned with relative holdings.

The former are patterned conceptions, while the latter are end-state theories. Thus, we can identify three main categories of theories of justice, namely theories dealing with (i) end-states, (ii) patterns and (iii) entitlements. Theories of types (i) and (ii) are structural in nature, while type (iii) theories are procedural.

More precisely, end-states are concerned with the structural features of the distribution of holdings. They tell us to look at the distributional matrix and assess whether the distribution satisfies certain structural constraints, whether holdings are distributed in the right proportions. Patterned accounts of justice, on the contrary, require us to take into consideration additional features that go beyond the information contained within the distributional matrix. They require us to assess some independent dimension or set of dimensions according to which distributions should be patterned. These accounts thereby connect the structural features of the distribution with structural features of another variable or a set of variables that is taken to provide a pattern. We can give a more fine-grained classification by distinguishing theories that appeal to a single dimension from those that make use of multiple dimensions and then differentiate the latter according to the ways in which the dimensions are weighted or ordered. Moreover, patterned accounts can be divided into historical and ahistorical theories, depending upon whether the dimension used for structuring the holdings is a historical dimension or not. When dealing with accounts that pattern along multiple dimensions, mixed theories also become possible in that some of the dimensions are historical while others are ahistorical.

Thus, end-state and patterned theories are different kinds of structural conceptions of justice. End-state conceptions

can be considered as limiting cases of patterned conceptions. In the case of such theories the structuring principle
or pattern is not provided by some independent dimension.
They do not require us to structure the distribution of
holdings according to certain independent characteristics,
but to structure it according to structural principles that
only appeal to features of the distributional matrix. This
means that we can lump the various end-state and patterned conceptions together since they are all structural
in nature. This is important for Nozick because it enables
him to argue in favour of the entitlement view by criticizing structural conceptions of justice per se. He can reject
all theories that are structural in nature, without having
to deal with particular theories on a case by case basis. The
rejection of structural theories then implies that we should
instead adopt a procedural account that specifies the processes that determine whether a distribution is just.

Nozick's entitlement theory is, of course, such a procedural conception. It is a historical account that looks at the
processes by which a distribution has arisen. It does not
specify any structural features, but is purely procedural in
nature. The entitlement theory does not specify any natural
dimension along which distributions should be patterned.
Nor does it structure holdings according to independently
given structuring principles. Instead, the principles of
justice specify processes whereby just entitlements can be
generated, without specifying how things have to turn out.
Whatever satisfies the principles is just, no matter how
holdings end up being distributed. The sets of holdings
generated in accordance with Nozick's principles of justice
are likely to have many strands of different patterns run-
ning through them. This is because many of the individual
transactions that give rise to any particular set of holdings
will be based on particular patterns. However, there is no

overarching pattern to which it is likely to conform or to which it needs to conform. The conformity or lack of conformity to any such patterns is of no relevance to the justice of the set of holdings, to the question whether people are entitled to the holdings that they do possess. 'The system of entitlements is defensible when constituted by the individual aims of individual transactions. No overarching aim is needed, no distributional pattern is required' (p. 159).

An important feature of the entitlement theory is that entitlements at a time do not depend on what other people are entitled to at that time. 'The entitlement principle of justice in holdings satisfies both the deletion and the addition conditions; the entitlement principle is non-organic and aggregative' (p. 210). This is because entitlements are not based on proportions or ratios, but on historical processes. Having been legitimately acquired is sufficient for being entitled to the holding, independently of whatever might be happening elsewhere. Hence, neither the addition of new people into the distribution, nor the deletion of people already in the distribution in any way alters entitlements. In short, entitlements are not extrinsically sensitive (except insofar as we are dealing with the proviso and its 'historical shadow'). They do not depend upon how many other people there are or what holdings those other people have.

Most patterned principles of justice, however, do not satisfy either the addition condition or both conditions. This means that a change in how many other people there are can change the justness of the distribution. On such accounts, a person's legitimately acquired holdings can suddenly fail to comply with the pattern, simply as a result of the deletion or addition of other people in the distribution. That person's holdings will accordingly suddenly become unjust without him (or anyone else) having done anything wrong. A further implication of this extrinsic sensitivity is that the justice of holdings depends on the comparison class. Thus, a distribution within a society may conform to the structural conditions of justice, while a set which contains this distribution, such as the global distribution, may fail to do so. This raises the difficult question for pattern theorists as to which comparison class is the correct one, a difficult question that the entitlement theorist does not have to face since entitlements are not affected by what happens elsewhere.

Nozick criticizes patterned conceptions for their implicit assumption that goods are up for grabs, that their status is as if they had come into existence ex nihilo. He argues that it is not the case that we have goods and then need to distribute them in accordance with some pattern. We are not dealing with a situation where manna comes from heaven and then has to be distributed. There is no social pie that needs to be divided and allocated to different people. The entitlement theory strongly rejects the separation of production and distribution. Manna does not fall from heaven. Instead, things have to be produced. Production, however, gives rise to entitlements that preclude the distribution of the produced goods. Holdings come into existence with entitlements attached to them. An object produced by someone is not available for distribution since that person is entitled to it (assuming that he was entitled to the resources used in the production). The differential contributions to the 'social pie' give rise to differential entitlements (cf. p. 160 & p. 198).

Against patterns

The main argument against end-state and patterned accounts of justice is that liberty upsets patterns. Any pattern that is imposed can only be kept up by prohibiting acts that undermine the pattern or by constantly redistributing to bring the pattern back into existence. Nozick wants to argue that in order to bring about and maintain a patterned distribution, one has to 'forbid capitalist acts between consenting adults' (p. 163). To illustrate this point, Nozick gives his famous Wilt Chamberlain example.

We begin with the pattern theorist's favoured distribution D1. This may be a distribution in accordance with need, an equal distribution or the implementation of some other pattern. Wilt Chamberlain then signs a contract with a basketball team, specifying that 25 cents from the price of each ticket will go to him. During the course of the season, one million people come to watch Wilt Chamberlain, happily paying the ticket price since they get a great deal of satisfaction out of seeing him play. At the end of the season, we have a new distribution D2 in which Chamberlain will end up with $250,000 from the ticket sales and will accordingly be much richer than other people.

Now, Nozick asks whether D2 is just. 'If D1 was a just distribution, and people voluntarily moved from it to D2, transferring parts of their shares they were given under D1 (what was it for if not to do something with?), isn't D2 also just?' (p. 161). Prima facie, it seems that D2 is a perfectly just distribution. It arose out of a completely just situation, namely D1, by voluntary means. Individuals voluntarily decided to transfer some of the resources they possessed under D1, thereby bringing about D2. While seeming innocuous, this transformation from D1 to D2 will be troublesome to pattern theorists. This is because there is no guarantee that the voluntary transactions of individuals are going to preserve the pattern. In fact, it is highly likely that these voluntary transfers will upset the pattern.

Thus, we started from a distribution that was in accordance with a particular pattern and by means of voluntary steps arrived at a distribution that no longer fits the pattern. Accordingly, we can see that liberty upsets patterns. 'To maintain a pattern one must either continually interfere to stop people from transferring resources as they wish to, or continually (or periodically) interfere to take from some persons resources that others for some reason chose to transfer to them' (p. 163).

The Wilt Chamberlain example raises two clusters of problems for the pattern theorist. On the one hand, the advocate of a patterned account of justice must explain what went wrong in this example. We began with a just starting point and moved by apparently just steps, given that they were all voluntary, to an unjust outcome. The pattern theorist needs to explain where injustice crept in. He needs to give an account as to why the outcome is unjust. No plausible story seems to be forthcoming and it appears counter-intuitive to judge D2 to be unjust. In particular, it is not clear what about D2 it is that is unacceptable. Nothing seems to have gone wrong and no one can complain about D2. All transactions leading to D2 were voluntary and were effected from a just starting point. The people performing the actions cannot complain since they voluntarily brought them about. If they are unhappy with the outcome, then they have no one to blame but themselves, which means that no injustice has occurred, no injustice has been done to them.

The pattern theorist might try to argue that, while those engaged in the interactions have no cause for complaint, these actions can have negative impacts on third parties, resulting in an injustice. However, there does not seem to be any basis for complaint by a third party. They still have the same share as before (cf. pp. 161–162). No one has been made worse off by the exchanges since we are concerned with Pareto improvements. Pareto improvements are harmless and it is strange to claim that they can be the source of injustice. That is, we are dealing with voluntary exchanges whereby no one is made worse off. As a result of the exchange, it simply is the case that some people are better off than they were before the exchange took place, but this does not happen at the expense of anyone else. There are no negative effects on third parties, which means that they have no cause for complaint.

On the other hand, the pattern theorist must impose restrictions on the behaviour of individuals and must argue for continuous interference. In order to preserve the pattern, there must be a significant reduction in the range of permissible options. This seems inappropriate and unjustified. Justice should not require us to interfere with liberty in such a significant way. In addition, the imposition of such restrictions is highly costly since it amounts to prohibiting large numbers of mutually beneficial exchanges. The pattern theorist will have to rule out many Pareto improvements and deem them unacceptable. The need to prohibit capitalist acts among consenting adults and the high costs imposed on society as a result of prohibiting many mutually beneficial exchanges are deeply troubling and counterintuitive consequences of patterned theories of justice.

To preserve a pattern, voluntary transfers that are going to undermine the pattern must be prohibited. Since most uses of the resources are likely to upset the pattern, there is hardly anything that can be done with the resources. That is, there is only a limited number of possibilities of employing resources without upsetting patterns, which means that the pattern theorist has to put into place a significant number of restrictions and prohibitions. This then gives rise to the question as to what the reason was for giving the resources to people under D1 in the first place. If they are not allowed to freely exchange and transfer the resources that have been distributed to them, then what was the point of bringing about D1 at all? Being allocated resources that one cannot freely employ is not particularly appealing. As Nozick notes: 'Patterned distributional principles do not give people what entitlement principles do, only better distributed. For they do not give the right to choose what to do with what one has' (p. 167). The patterned theories only consider people as recipients of resources, not as agents who make use of them. Thus, in the same way that patterned principles do not look at where things come from and how they were produced, so they do not look at what things are used for. They ignore both the production as well as the utilization of goods, focusing instead merely on the distribution of possessions.

From this we can see that the position advocated by the defender of patterns appears to be to some extent self-undermining. His theory is partly self-defeating in that the restrictions and interferences required for maintaining the pattern undermine some of the original justification for implementing the pattern in the first place. A pattern theorist demands that we distribute R in accordance with pattern P. It may be asked why R should be distributed, why R is considered to be fit for distribution, why holdings of R are subject to the distributive pattern P. A reasonable response will be that R should be distributed because it is of value, because it can be gainfully employed. The gainful employability of R is what gives a point to distributing it.

Now, the Chamberlain example shows that pattern theorists end up in a situation where R is distributed to individuals according to some pattern but where these individuals are not allowed to use it in a way that upsets the pattern, which means that there is not much that they can do with it. R is distributed but cannot be utilized except in a restricted manner. People are given resources that they cannot use as they deem fit. However, if the resources cannot be utilized in a gainful manner, then there is not much point in distributing them in the first place. If most ways of gainfully utilizing the resource are prohibited, then there is not much value in possessing it and there is consequently not much point in distributing it.

Hence, the very benefits which warranted the distribution of R in the first place cannot be properly gained from having received R. This is because the distributive principle P rules out the employment of R in a way that upsets the pattern. The reasons for distributing R to begin with, the reasons for treating R as a resource that is to be subjected to P, are partly undermined by distributing R in accordance with P. We treat R as worthy of distribution because it can be gainfully employed. Distributing it in accordance with P, however, precludes many ways of gainfully employing it, thereby to some extent undermining the rationale for distributing it in the first place.

After having presented the Wilt Chamberlain example, Nozick goes on to provide further arguments against patterned conceptions of justice and thereby against the need for a more-than-minimal state to achieve distributive justice. He argues that it is not only the case that the preservation of patterns requires the prohibition of many capitalist acts among consenting adults or the continual interference and redistribution of resources. In addition, the implementation of patterns often requires some form of taxation of income from labour and such taxation is on a par

with forced labour. Nozick argues that 'patterned principles of distributive justice involve appropriating the actions
of other persons. Seizing the results of someone's labor is
equivalent to seizing hours from him and directing him
to carry on various activities' (p. 172). Taxation involves
taking the product of one's labour. Taking the income of
n hours of work from a person amounts to taking n hours
from that person. It is like forcing the person to work
n hours for a purpose he has not chosen.

Given that income taxation involves changing the incentive structure in such a way that people have to work
n hours more to achieve their goals, it may be objected
that it is not a form of forced labour since it gives people
the choice how much to work and what kind of work to
do. In other words, it can be objected that taxation only
reduces the range of alternatives and it does not involve
forcing people to do particular things. Moreover, if income
taxation only applies to earnings above a certain amount,
then taxation can be avoided altogether. However, Nozick
replies that income taxation does involve forcing people
since it is a case of coercion that involves a violation of
the side constraint against aggression. 'The fact that others
intentionally intervene, in violation of a side constraint
against aggression, to threaten force to limit the alternatives . . . makes the taxation system one of forced labor and
distinguishes it from other cases of limited choices which
are not forcings' (p. 169).

Thus, taxation on income from labour involves forcing
people to work for purposes that they have not chosen.
The implementation of patterned principles then gives
people a claim on the labour of other people. This is
because it gives them a claim on a certain portion of the

total social product that has been produced by the labour of individuals. To give people an enforceable claim on the product of the labour of other people amounts to giving people partial ownership in other people. It amounts to a claim on their work, a claim on their time. This contravenes the thesis of self-ownership. 'End-state and most patterned principles of distributive justice institute (partial) ownership by others of people and their actions and labor. These principles involve a shift from the classical liberal's notion of self-ownership to a notion of (partial) property rights in *other* people' (p. 172).

In addition, Nozick notes that taxation on income from labour fails to be neutral since it discriminates against people with expensive tastes. Nozick contrasts the situation of someone who prefers seeing a movie with someone who prefers looking at a sunset. The first person will have to work to earn money for the ticket, while the second person will not have to earn any extra money. Taxation on income from labour will ensure that the former person will have to work extra to satisfy his preferences, while the latter person can avoid the income tax without any prejudice to his happiness. Those who need to earn more money to satisfy their desires will have to pay more income tax which means that they will have to work more for purposes that others have set for them. Those who do not have to work much to satisfy their desires, on the contrary, can easily avoid this burden. Yet, there seems to be no principled reason for discriminating against those who have expensive tastes. 'Why should we treat the man whose happiness requires certain material goods or services differently from the man whose preferences and desires make such goods unnecessary for his happiness?' (p. 170).

Moral luck, equality and entitlements

One of the most forceful objections to the entitlement theory is that this conception of justice is undermined by the arbitrariness of natural assets and social circumstances. In his discussion of the 'system of natural liberty', which is similar to the entitlement theory, John Rawls notes that this system is to be rejected because 'it permits distributive shares to be improperly influenced by [natural and social contingencies, which are] so arbitrary from a moral point of view' (quoted in Nozick: 1974, p. 213). The argument is that sets of holdings under an entitlement regime are significantly influenced by natural endowments and social circumstances, which are morally arbitrary. In other words, what people end up with is largely determined by morally arbitrary factors. Accordingly, Rawls claims that we should nullify the effects of natural endowments and social contingencies.

Nozick's response begins by noting that there is a perspicuous absence in Rawls's discussion of the choices that people make. While natural endowments and social circumstances may be arbitrary, it does not straightforwardly follow that what we do with these endowments and how we develop them is arbitrary. Because the choice situation is arbitrary does not automatically imply that the choices made within this situation are equally arbitrary. In response, it may be suggested that the choices themselves are determined by the natural and social contingencies and that how people use their endowments is shaped by these contingencies. However, Nozick replies: 'This line of argument can succeed in blocking the introduction of a person's autonomous choices and actions (and their results) only by attributing *everything* noteworthy about the person completely to certain sorts of "external" factors' (p. 214).

To claim that choices are equally arbitrary as the natural and social contingencies amounts to denigrating the autonomy, dignity and worth of individuals. If individuals cannot claim responsibility for their choices, then there does not seem to be any room left for treating them as moral agents, which is contrary to the spirit of Rawls's own theory.

The claim that natural endowments and social circumstances are arbitrary from a moral point of view can be appealed to in two different ways. 'Whereas the positive argument attempts to establish that the distributive effects of natural differences ought to be nullified, the negative one, by merely rebutting *one* argument that the differences oughtn't to be nullified, leaves open the possibility that (for other reasons) the differences oughtn't be nullified' (p. 216).

A positive argument attempts to establish that differences resulting from morally arbitrary factors should be neutralized. Such an argument starts with a premise as to how holdings should be distributed and then points out that natural differences do not meet these standards. It thence concludes that distributive differences deriving from these natural differences should be nullified. Nozick identifies a number of premises that could be used in a positive argument, namely (i) that persons should morally deserve their holdings, (ii) that holdings should be distributed in accordance with a pattern that is not morally arbitrary, or (iii) that holdings should be equal unless there is a moral reason to the contrary. The problem with positive arguments is that these premises are simply assumed and not in any way supported. Moreover, all of these premises amount to patterned conceptions of justice and are as such subject to Nozick's critiques. In the absence of

an argument to the effect that holdings should be distributed according to some pattern or to the effect that equality is to be the default position, the arbitrariness of natural
differences can at best feature in a negative argument.

A negative argument tries to undermine an argument
that attempts to justify distributive differences resulting
from natural differences. If someone attempts to claim
that people deserve their differential holdings on the basis
that these holdings derive from their talents, then the
negative argument undermines this claim. It does this by
pointing out that talents are not deserved given that they
are a matter of brute luck. Accordingly, the negative argument does not provide any support for nullifying or neu-
tralizing distributive differences. It simply states that such
differences are not supported by considerations of desert.
In the end this leads to a neutral position, whereby the
distributive differences seem to be neither justified nor
unjustified.

In his response to the negative argument Nozick draws
our attention again to the important distinction between
desert and entitlement. There are many things we are entitled to that we do not deserve and there are things we do
deserve to which we are not entitled. Desert and entitlement are different notions and, according to Nozick, distributive justice is concerned with entitlement and not
desert. Desert is a dimension that can govern patterns, but
patterns are to be rejected as bases for distribution. While
he takes the negative argument seriously as a critique of
theories that appeal to desert, he argues that it is ineffective against the entitlement theory. That is, the negative
argument only undermines certain patterned conceptions,
but has no bearing when it comes to the entitlement
theory.

Since we can have entitlements without desert, we can have differential entitlements without having differential deserts. An important consequence is that there is no need to deserve that which is utilized in acquiring an entitlement. We only need to be entitled to those things that are used in this way and while we may not deserve our talents, we are entitled to them, given that we accept the thesis of self-ownership. To deny that we are entitled to our talents would be tantamount to denying self-ownership. 'Whether or not people's natural assets are arbitrary from a moral point of view, they are entitled to them, and to what flows from them' (p. 226). Entitlements over our talents allow us to gain entitlements over other things, even though we might not deserve either our talents or the things we have acquired. Since justice is concerned with entitlements and not with deserts, no injustices arise in this way.

Moreover, not only is it the case that we can be entitled to differential holdings without deserving those holdings, there is a good case to be made to the effect that desert is possible after all since desert need not go all the way down. Otherwise, desert would be entirely impossible. In fact, Nozick notes that not only desert would be impossible, but that there would not be anything that would retain moral relevance. If something's being arbitrary from a moral point of view were to automatically imply its moral irrelevance, then our very existence would be morally irrelevant. 'If nothing of moral significance could flow from what was arbitrary, then no particular person's existence could be of moral significance' (p. 226, footnote).

Instead, it seems that moral significance can emerge. The things giving rise to moral significance may obtain for arbitrary reasons without thereby losing their moral significance. Nozick points out that the claim that something is arbitrary from a moral point of view is ambiguous. 'It might mean that there is no moral reason why the fact ought to be that way, or it might mean that the fact's being that way is of no moral significance and has no moral consequences' (p. 227). Only the former reading applies to our existence and our talents. While there is no moral reason to the effect that we should exist or that we should have those talents which we do have, this does not undermine the fact that our existence and our talents are of moral significance and have moral consequences.

The minimal state as an inspiring utopia

Nozick argues that a minimal state can be justified and that anything that goes beyond such a minimum is illegitimate. This understanding of the state is primarily negative, placing restrictions on the functions of the state, rather than identifying a positive and worthy role that it should fulfil. Nonetheless, Nozick believes this view of the state not only to be morally right but also to be inspiring. According to him, a minimal state is an inspiring utopia towards which we should strive.

The account of utopia is not only supposed to render the minimal state more interesting and attractive, but also to constitute an independent argument in favour of the minimal state. It is not merely a supplement, but an argument for libertarianism in its own right. Nozick claims that there is a convergence of the results of the different parts of the book. In the final part, the minimal state is not advocated on the basis of moral arguments that appeal to individual rights. Instead, it is shown to be an inspiring form of social organization that can respect the diversity and individuality of different people, enabling everyone to live in accordance with their conception of the good life.

This independent role of the framework of utopia is particularly important given the absence of a detailed and well worked out foundation of Nozick's moral philosophy. The arguments for the minimal state considered as a framework for utopia do not rely on the contentious understanding of rights that Nozick appeals to in the prior parts. Nozick thinks that even those who reject the starting point of individual rights should advocate the minimal state insofar as it amounts to a framework for utopia that permits different people to form varying communities and attempt to realize their respective utopian conceptions in a peaceful manner.

The best possible world

Nozick begins his discussion by examining the notion of utopia. Utopia is the best possible world. It is the ideal state of affairs. Since we are concerned with political philosophy, the question of what classifies as the best possible world becomes a question of institutional design or institutional evaluation, namely the question of which set of institutions would count as the best. While utopia is the best possible world, the question arises for whom this world is the best. What is best for me need not be best for you. Utopia should not simply be the best world for a particular person or certain group of people, but should rather be the best possible world for each of us.

The question then is: What is the best possible world for each of us? Nozick provides an answer to this question by devising a possible worlds model whereby a person can imagine a possible world and all the people therein.

Each person in that world has the same powers of imagining and is given the choice to stay in that world or imagine his own world. This process is then repeated again and again. If stable worlds should arise, then these worlds will have the property of being such that no person in that world can imagine a better world (that he believes would also be stable). This surely fits our understanding of utopia. A utopian world is a world which is such that there is no other world anyone would rather be in. 'If there are stable worlds, each of them satisfies one very desirable description by virtue of the way the worlds have been set up; namely, *none* of the inhabitants of the world can *imagine* an alternative world they would rather live in' (p. 299).

Having described this abstract model, Nozick then tries to apply it to the actual world. In reality we are, of course, not able to move from world to world, but are restricted to the world we happen to be in. Nonetheless, we can find a real-world analogue for these imagined possible worlds, namely associations. An association is a collection of people subject to certain rules and is thus similar to a possible world. People can create associations and leave them to create new associations or join existing ones, which is similar to the procedure of imagining new worlds or joining existing worlds. It should be noted though that there are a number of differences between the model and its real-world analogue, such as the existence of transaction costs involved in moving from one community to another and the fact that communities impinge upon another whereas possible worlds are isolated.

While there are these disanalogies, it nonetheless seems that the analogies are strong enough for the possible worlds model to have explanatory relevance. In particular, it seems that we can transfer the idea that a stable association will be such that no member of that association would rather be in any other association, given that people are free to create, exit and join communities. Utopia then is achieved if all associations satisfy this condition. 'In *our* actual world, what corresponds to the model of possible worlds is a wide and diverse range of communities . . . a society in which utopian experimentation can be tried, different styles of life can be lived, and alternative visions of the good can be individually and jointly pursued' (p. 307).

Individuality, diversity and the minimal state

Thus, Nozick conceives of utopia as a diverse collection of stable associations. This is in conflict with traditional utopian conceptions that advance the claim that there is one best possible world, one stable association. Nozick rejects this view and instead conceives of utopia as a framework that encompasses a large number of different communities.

On the one hand, we need a plurality of communities because people differ. Given the vast diversity of human beings, it becomes questionable whether there is one best way to live one's life that is applicable to everyone. Individuals differ significantly and it seems that there is not one best way of living that applies equally to all of them. There are different best lives for different people. This is a fact that is not respected by traditional utopian theories. They simply assume that their conception of the good applies to everyone. This, however, is inappropriate and the utopian vision does not turn out to be the best possible world for each of us, but only for a small sub-section of society. 'The conclusion to draw is that there will not be *one* kind of community existing and one kind of life led in utopia. Utopia will consist of utopias, of many different and divergent communities in which people lead different kinds of lives under different institutions' (pp. 311–312). We thus need a range of different communities so that different people can have their best possible world.

On the other hand, even if one conception of the good life were the best, we would still need a plurality of communities to identify what that best way of life would be. Even if we assume that there is one substantive utopia, there is still the problem of finding out what this is. Not only is it the case that traditional utopian theories do not adequately take into account the diversity of individuals. In addition, they face serious epistemological problems. Given the complexity of human life, the claim of having identified the optimal way of living seems downright presumptuous. Nozick argues that the framework of utopia can be seen as an excellent mechanism for discovering the best way of life. What makes it a good mechanism for overcoming these epistemological problems is that the framework is a filtering device rather than a design device.

Design devices directly specify the characteristics of the intended outcome. They specify what the product is supposed to be like. We can see that it is hard to come up with an account of all the characteristics that the best community must have. Given the vast complexity and diversity of human beings and their interactions, it follows that there are so many factors to be taken into consideration that the task of designing the perfect society becomes practically impossible. Accordingly, one should not try to make use of design devices, but rather turn to filtering devices.

Filtering devices work by means of various filters that weed out inappropriate products from a large set of alternatives. A filtering device has two components, namely one that specifies how alternatives are to be generated and one that specifies the filtering processes that operate on the generated alternatives. Ideally, we want a process in which the alternatives that are generated, as well as the filters that operate on these alternatives, become more and more sophisticated as the process goes on. We thereby end up with an evolutionary process in which a large range of different communities are designed and then tested. Such a system of experimentation and of trial and error will allow us to identify which conceptions are feasible and worth pursuing. 'The operation of the framework for utopia we present here thus realizes the advantages of a filtering process incorporating mutually improving inter-action between the filter and the surviving products of the generating process, so that the quality of generated and nonrejected products improves' (p. 317). The framework allows us to continuously improve the communities we are living in, rather than expecting us to set down once and for all the ideal community.

Thus, we have seen that traditional utopian accounts are problematic because of the fact that individuals differ significantly which suggests that there is no objectively best life that fits everyone. Moreover, we have seen that, even if we were to assume that there is such a thing as a best life, we would not be able to identify it by means of design devices. For Nozick, the adequate response to this predica-ment does not consist in giving up utopian theorizing. Instead, one should move to a further level of abstraction. In particular, this involves identifying what is the common ground among various non-coercive utopias. In this way, one can provide a meta-utopia, a framework for utopia within which the particular utopian visions of different people can be realized. Nozick then argues that this frame-work is embodied by the minimal state. The minimal state retains what is good and inspiring about utopianism, without being prone to the difficulties that particular utopian visions face.

In order to achieve utopia, what we need to do is to implement the conditions that are requisite for having associations that are such that no one would rather be in another association. This is done by ensuring that people have the freedom to leave associations, to experiment and to create new communities. People must be able to try out different ways of living and to decide for themselves which association they would like to be a member of. These functions are, of course, the functions fulfilled by the minimal state. The minimal state provides the framework for utopia, the framework within which each of us is able to pursue his or her own utopia. 'Utopia is a framework for utopias, a place where people are at liberty to join together voluntarily to pursue and attempt to realize their own vision of the good life in the ideal community but where no one can *impose* his own utopian vision upon others. The utopian society is the society of utopianism' (p. 312).

This framework is compatible with a wide variety of utopian conceptions. In particular, it does not require that associations be governed by capitalist or libertarian norms, but allows associations that are based on non-libertarian and even anti-libertarian utopias. As Nozick notes 'in a free society people may contract into various restrictions which the government may not legitimately impose upon them' (p. 320). There is no requirement for associations to adopt libertarian norms in their internal dealings. All that is required is that membership be voluntary. It is only the external dealings with other associations that are governed by the norms of the libertarian framework. Accordingly, associations may do things that states may not do.

While states may not make use of redistributive or pater- nalistic policies, voluntary associations can implement such policies. That is, voluntary associations can impose requirements on their members that states could not impose on their citizens.

Ensuring that different people can pursue their own utopian schemes requires us to rule out the use of coer- cion to realize utopian visions. Nozick distinguishes three kinds of utopian views, namely (i) imperialistic views that condone or require the use of force in getting other peo- ple to subscribe to their views, (ii) missionary views that want others to adopt their views but require that this adop- tion be voluntary and not forced and (iii) existential views that are neutral with respect to the views held by others. It is only the first kind that is in conflict with the frame- work of utopia. Imperialistic utopian views countenance the attempt to forcefully impose their particular vision of society on other people. The use or threat of force is, how- ever, ruled out by the framework. This means that the framework excludes the realization of imperialistic utopias by coercive means. Only the voluntary adoption or rejec- tion of life-styles and the voluntary joining as well as exit- ing of communities is permitted by the framework. Both missionary and existential accounts are fully compatible with this framework since they respect the requirement that the choice of life-style be voluntary. This is because missionary conceptions attempt to convince other people to freely adopt their conception and join their community, while existential conceptions hold a neutral stance towards other communities since, for them, all that matters is that they themselves follow their vision of society.

For Nozick then the minimal state is not inspiring by what it does, but rather by what it allows, by what it enables to take place. It is a society that evolves within the confines of a minimal state that is inspiring, rather than the minimal state itself. Such a state allows for the coexistence of widely diverging views of human flourishing. It does not specify a blueprint to which society has to conform, but allows individuals to live their lives as they see fit. Moreover, what is also inspiring is the moral outlook underlying the commitment to the minimal state. It is the dignity and autonomy of individuals that stands behind the inviolable rights that the minimal state is supposed to protect. This gives rise to the ideal of a non-coercive society in which the dignity of individuals is respected. In such a society, individuals can freely act and decide how to shape their lives.

Beyond *Anarchy, State, and Utopia*

After the publication of *Anarchy, State, and Utopia*, Nozick did not write any other substantial work on political philosophy and did not respond to any of the criticisms that were directed against his theory. Instead, we only get occasional comments and observations on issues relating to political theory, some of which have been taken as indications of a recantation of his commitment to libertarianism. For example, in *The Examined Life* Nozick makes several remarks critical of his earlier libertarian views. 'The libertarian position I once propounded now seems to me seriously inadequate, in part because it did not fully knit the humane considerations and joint cooperative activities it left room for more closely into its fabric. It neglected the symbolic importance of an official political concern with issues or problems' (Nozick: 1989, pp. 286–287). Similarly, in *The Nature of Rationality*, Nozick says that '[t]he political philosophy presented in *Anarchy, State, and Utopia* ignored the importance to us of joint and official serious symbolic statement and expression of our social ties and concern and hence . . . is inadequate' (Nozick: 1993, p. 32).

More precisely, his dissatisfaction with the radical libertarianism presented in *Anarchy, State, and Utopia* derives from considerations regarding symbolic value and symbolic meaning. Nozick's account of rationality includes a concern for symbolic utility. He identifies a rule for rational decision making which he calls 'maximizing decision-value', whereby the decision-value consists of causal, evidential and symbolic utility. It is symbolic utility that was ignored in his earlier writings and that is supposedly in conflict with radical libertarianism. 'The libertarian view looked solely at the purpose of government, not at its *meaning*; hence, it took an unduly narrow view of purpose, too' (Nozick: 1989, p. 288).

'The point is not simply to accomplish the particular purpose – that might be done through private contributions alone – or to get the others to pay too – that could occur through stealing the necessary funds from them – but also to speak solemnly in everyone's name, in the name of the society, about what it holds dear' (Nozick: 1989, p. 298). Thus, Nozick came to the view that political institutions can play an important role in that they express and symbolize commitments. Political institutions do not simply perform certain functions and achieve certain goals but, in doing so, have an expressive nature. To publicly adopt a purpose involves the expression of a certain commitment and such expressions have value that needs to be taken into consideration. It is the symbolic value of joint commitments that libertarians have ignored when assessing the value and role of political institutions.

The question now arises to what extent this recognition of the symbolic value of politics is in conflict with and undermines the libertarianism that was advocated in *Anarchy, State, and Utopia*. It seems that the conflict is relatively minimal. Considerations pertaining to symbolic value only affect certain extreme cases, leaving the core of libertarianism intact. Rather than undermining libertarianism, the recognition of symbolic value leads at most to a milder form of libertarianism. That is, the symbolic value of politics is not fundamentally at odds with the main thrust of libertarianism. In fact, the cases where symbolic value has a significant role to play are primarily cases that pertain to the importance of freedom. Nozick claims that considerations based on symbolic value can be invoked to favour anti-discrimination laws and limits on freedom of speech and assembly, i.e. against hate speech (cf. Nozick: 1989, p. 291). He argues that we need to positively express the value of freedom and our commitment to the dignity of individuals. This means that we must prohibit practices that conflict with and directly undermine freedom or that denigrate the dignity of individuals. We are thus not dealing with an independent constraint placed upon the rights and freedoms of individuals, but with a constraint that derives from a commitment to those very rights and freedoms.

This interpretation is supported by Nozick's statement made in an interview conducted by Julian Sanchez in 2001. There he said that he never stopped calling himself a libertarian. 'What I was really saying in *The Examined Life* was that I was no longer as *hardcore* a libertarian as I had been before. But the rumors of my deviation (or apostasy!) from libertarianism were much exaggerated. I think [*Invariances*] makes clear the extent to which I still

am within the general framework of libertarianism, especially the ethics chapter and its section on the "Core
Principle of Ethics".'

Thus, there does not seem to be a fundamental conflict
and it appears that certain forms of libertarianism can
be reconciled with a commitment to symbolic value. Nonetheless, Nozick's position on symbolic value seems to be
problematic from the viewpoint of *Anarchy, State, and
Utopia*. It is only in conjunction with a modification of the
underlying moral theory that considerations regarding
symbolic value could lead Nozick to change his views.

First, it should be noted that invoking symbolic value
does not in any way affect conclusions established on the
basis of individual rights. Since rights are considered as
side constraints, it follows that they clearly trump symbolic
concerns. If taxation involves a rights-violation, then taxation is morally illegitimate even if the resources collected
through taxation are utilized to express certain commitments in a way that possesses symbolic value. If someone
has a right to express hateful speech, then it is illegitimate
to prevent that person from expressing himself even if
this prevention has symbolic value since it symbolizes our
commitment to the value and dignity of individuals. As
mentioned at the beginning of this chapter, moral philosophy determines the boundaries of political philosophy.
Symbolic value may play an important role in assessing
the value of public as well as private actions within these
boundaries. However, it cannot justify the transgression
of these boundaries. This means that a commitment to
symbolic value is on its own insufficient to moderate the
libertarian account of the role of the state that Nozick
developed in *Anarchy, State, and Utopia*. Only in conjunction with a weakening of the status of individual rights,

resulting from the abandoning of a strict Kantian theory, could this moderation take place.

Second, while there may be a role for government that has been ignored, namely to express certain commitments the expression of which possesses symbolic value, Nozick has not made it clear that there are no private alternatives for this role. That is, the expression of these commitments does not seem to exclusively pertain to the government. In fact, it appears that voluntary expression is much more powerful than coerced expression. Moreover, Nozick seems to be relying on an overly optimistic understanding of politics and the public realm in his remarks about symbolic value.

While not returning to political philosophy, Nozick did work on issues about ethics, in particular in *Philosophical Explanations* and in *Invariances*. Particularly noteworthy is the abandonment of the broadly Kantian account of morality that we saw in *Anarchy, State, and Utopia*. Instead of working out the details of his Kantian approach to ethics, he decided to try out various different approaches to morality. In *Philosophical Explanations* there is a great emphasis on value understood as organic unity, while he favours an evolutionary approach in his last book *Invariances*. The abandonment of Kantianism somewhat softened his libertarianism. While still remaining a libertarian, his views were no longer quite as radical and as strict anymore. Giving up a Kantian position leads to a less absolutist account, whereby rights are no longer understood as side constraints that place rigid restrictions on actions, thereby making more room for various other values.

3

Reception and Influence

Anarchy, State, and Utopia has had a significant impact and still influences the way political philosophy is done. Together with John Rawls's *A Theory of Justice*, it has largely shaped political philosophy for the last 35 years and continues to be one of the classics of political theory.

The book received instant acclaim due to the controversial nature of Nozick's theory and due to the clarity and strength of the arguments that Nozick provides in support of his unconventional views and his criticisms of the mainstream. As Steiner notes, 'this book is the best piece of sustained analytical argument in political philosophy to have appeared in a very long time. Moreover it is, in its way, an extremely moving book, not the least because of the engaging manner in which it is written' (Steiner: 1977, p. 120).

While Nozick's work is much respected, its reception has been largely critical. Waldron nicely describes the reaction to the publication as 'universally hostile acclaim' (Waldron: 1982, p. 1277). The book is held in high regard and widely praised but the theory Nozick propounds is mostly rejected. The secondary literature is vast but for the most part critical. The debate is rather one-sided and it is rarely the case that Nozick's side is taken. Nozick himself did not contribute to this debate, but rather focused his attention on other philosophical issues. Moreover, there were not many other philosophers taking up and defending Nozick's views. Nozick has not produced a new school of thought. Unlike Rawls, he does not have many followers. This seems to be in line with what Nozick wanted to achieve. He wanted to get people to think about certain issues, to present interesting arguments and to challenge the received wisdom. He wanted to say something without saying last words.

The reason why it was so well received and why it generated so much discussion, despite the fact that the critiques were rarely answered, is that it poses a serious challenge to the mainstream. As we have seen, Nozick does not develop a monolithic system and does not engage in a foundational project. He is rather involved in trying out ideas, raising possibilities and criticizing the prevailing orthodoxy. Nozick sketches an alternative way of thinking about justice, while criticizing several fundamental assumptions held by the mainstream. Rather than providing a complete system of thought, Nozick presented many powerful objections to a number of widely accepted views. Accordingly, 'a great deal of Nozick's importance lies in his waking others from their dogmatic slumbers' (Wolff: 1991, p. 118).

As a result, the reception of *Anarchy, State, and Utopia* has been somewhat skewed so far in that most discussions amount to responses to Nozick's critiques. Most of those who engage with this book attempt to undermine or weaken Nozick's arguments against end-state or patterned conceptions of justice. Accordingly, there has been a disproportionate focus on the second part of *Anarchy, State, and Utopia*. It is Nozick's entitlement theory and historical conception of justice, his critique of Rawls and his defence of a Lockean theory of property that have received the most attention. This means that the larger picture has to some extent been underappreciated.

While the ideas discussed in the second part are highly significant contributions, the other parts of his work should not be neglected even though they are more exploratory in nature and deal with issues that are slightly tangential to mainstream concerns. Only once the work is considered as a whole is it possible to really appreciate its value not merely as a response to Rawls and as setting out an alternative to patterned conceptions of justice, but rather as a substantive and comprehensive approach to political philosophy. The critique of anarchism and the discussion of utopia are highly original contributions that should be appreciated in their own right. In particular, the account of utopia brings out the positive vision which underlies Nozick's project and which informs the rest of his book. Focusing solely on the critiques of the mainstream only gives us a partial picture.

This chapter constitutes an assessment of Nozick's impact on and significance for political philosophy. We will examine the way in which *Anarchy, State, and Utopia* was received, by giving an account of which aspects of the Nozickian project have been accepted, criticized or neglected. In the next chapter we will then assess the relevance of Nozick's political philosophy by determining which of his key arguments, approaches and positions have been shown to be problematic and which are still viable.

Critique of rights-based libertarianism

Nozick's political philosophy rests on a somewhat shaky moral basis that has not been properly worked out and defended. The absence of a basis for individual rights has been the target of many criticisms and a common attitude to *Anarchy, State, and Utopia* is that, as Nagel puts it, Nozick gives us 'libertarianism without foundations', that the Nozickian project lacks a solid moral basis and can as such be easily dismissed. Yet, this kind of critique is somewhat misguided since it misunderstands the purpose of Nozick's book. Nozick does not attempt to provide a foundational project that starts from self-evident and undeniable axioms and then builds up a moral and political theory leading to libertarian conclusions. Nozick is fully aware of the limitations of his arguments. 'This book does not present a precise theory of the moral basis of individual rights' (p. xiv; also cf. p. 9). Instead, he starts with the intuitively plausible view that individuals have rights and that these rights give rise to constraints on how other people may act. Nozick then works out what political philosophy follows from this plausible starting point, trying to show that a minimal state and nothing more than a minimal state can be justified given the constraints imposed by this understanding of individual rights.

Moreover, Nozick does provide some support in favour of a rights-based approach, even if it does not amount to a full-fledged defence of individual rights. He does not simply assert that individuals have rights and then leaves it at that. Instead, he appeals to the separateness and inviolability of persons, to the Kantian idea that individuals are ends and not means, as well as to the inadequacy of goal-directed, consequentialist theories, such as utilitarianism, to support his understanding of rights. Nozick also gives good arguments as to how one should conceive of rights, what status they have and what structure a rights-based theory should embody. In particular, these arguments establish that if one accepts a rights-based account, then one should understand rights as side constraints. Accordingly, we can see that Nozick's understanding of individual rights considered as side constraints is not baseless and unsupported. Nozick does adduce a number of convincing considerations in favour of his view, even though he does not provide a watertight foundation.

Furthermore, only some of Nozick's arguments for libertarianism depend upon this contested premise. His criticisms of Rawls's views and those of other liberal egalitarians are based on claims and theories accepted by the defenders of these views. These criticisms provide support to libertarianism insofar as one can arrive there by elimination, leaving some form of libertarianism as the default position. This is particularly clear when assessing the entitlement theory of justice. The distinction between procedural and end-state or patterned conceptions of justice is an exhaustive and exclusive distinction. This implies that adequate critiques of the latter views leave the entitlement theory as the sole competitor. If Nozick's critiques of structural theories of justice are sufficient to establish the entitlement theory, then the lack of secure foundations will to some extent turn out to be unproblematic. This is because one can then arrive at libertarianism by eliminative arguments, rather than by foundational arguments.

This style of argumentation can be found throughout *Anarchy, State, and Utopia*. Many of Nozick's arguments are internal criticisms of other positions that show that these positions are incoherent or somehow self-undermining and self-defeating. He is willing to base his arguments and critiques on the same assumptions as his opponents, rather than providing external criticisms that could be accused of begging the question. For example, Nozick accepts the stringency of individual rights and is willing to grant the anarchist an optimistic description of the state of nature. He attempts to derive the minimal state from a state of nature in which the behaviour of individuals is largely in conformity with the requirements of morality. Similarly, a number of his arguments against Rawls are based on the separateness of persons to which Rawls is also committed (though it is not always clear whether they have the same understanding of the separateness of persons or whether they merely use the same term). Likewise, Nozick's Wilt Chamberlain argument against patterned theories of justice takes as its starting point a patterned conception of justice and then shows how such a conception is self-undermining, given that the upholding of a pattern requires measures that are unacceptable to pattern theorist and that conflict with the aims that underlie the patterned conceptions.

Additionally, there is independent support for Nozick's libertarianism coming from his argument that the minimal state is a framework for utopia. The argument for the meta-utopia is not based on moral considerations and does not rely on contentious claims about individual rights. This again shows that not all justification for the minimal state has to proceed in a foundationalist manner. Getting the right result, namely an inspiring and realistic meta-utopia, provides an independent reason for accepting the minimal state and suggests that the premises appealed to in the other arguments are correct. That is, if the arguments are valid and the conclusion correct, then this suggests that the premises are also correct and that the arguments are consequently sound.

While most critics were content to point out the lack of secure foundations for individual rights, a number of people have attempted to provide detailed objections to Nozick's arguments. Scheffler, for example, criticizes the connection between libertarian rights and the meaning of life that Nozick attempts to establish. Scheffler argues that giving people negative rights may not be the best way to go about if one wants to guarantee that they are in a position to lead meaningful lives. He claims that 'if the capacity to live a meaningful life is a uniquely valuable characteristic, and if we say that beings with this characteristic have *rights*, in virtue of which there are constraints on the way others must behave, then presumably the function of the rights is to safeguard the ability of beings with this valuable characteristic to *develop it*' (Scheffler: 1981, pp. 158–159). Rather than focusing on negative rights, Scheffler thinks that the best way to ensure that people can live meaningful lives is by granting them welfare rights. 'If the meaning of life is our concern, then starvation, not taxation, is our worthy foe' (Scheffler: 1981, p. 161).

While Scheffler is right in pointing out that considerations pertaining to the meaning of life fit naturally into teleological conceptions of ethics that favour welfare rights, Nozick's invocation of the meaning of life has a fundamentally different character which ensures that Scheffler's objection does not constitute an internal criticism of Nozick's theory. In particular, according to Nozick the connection between individual rights and the meaning of life is not supposed to be based on the idea that having individual rights somehow gives one the capacity to live a meaningful life or that we have rights in order to be able to live meaningful lives. Rights are not means for ensuring that people can live meaningful lives, which is what Scheffler assumes in his favouring welfare rights over negative rights. It is not the case that living a meaningful life is the goal that is to be achieved and that rights are the means that permit us to attain this goal. Rather, it is in virtue of the fact that human beings are agents whose lives can have meaning that we need to respect their choices, that we have to let them decide how to live their lives. Human beings have the status of being ends in themselves, rather than mere means, because they have the capacity to live meaningful lives. As Nozick explains in his book *Philosophical Explanations*, rights arise if we have to be responsive to certain moral characteristics of other people whereby our compliance can be enforced. The relevant characteristic that gives rise to this ethical-pull is that of being a value-seeking self. It is the possession of the capacity to shape one's life that exerts a moral pull on us, requiring us to respect the autonomy of such a value-seeking self and to treat it as an end rather than as a mere means. Accordingly, rights derive from the possibility of meaningful living, rather than being means for achieving a meaningful life.

Against the legitimate state

Most criticisms of Nozick's arguments in favour of the legitimacy of a minimal state have come from libertarian anarchists. Writers such as Childs, Rothbard, Barnett and Mack have argued that Nozick is unable to meet the anarchist's challenge. Even the minimal state violates the rights of individuals and is accordingly illegitimate. Nozick's derivation of the state has been criticized on the basis that his claims about dominant protective agencies are inadequate and that his views about prohibition and compensation are in conflict with his understanding of rights as absolute side constraints.

In particular, it has been argued that Nozick's move to the dominant protective agency is problematic. He does not provide any substantive support for his claim that a dominant protective agency will emerge. While it seems correct that we will end up in a situation in which different agencies will be dominant in different geographical regions if agencies should decide to engage in armed conflicts in case they should disagree about how to settle disputes between their clients, this is not the most plausible account of the behaviour of protective agencies. An alternative and more likely option is that we end up with a stable situation in which different protective agencies compete peacefully with each other. In order to avoid violent conflicts, they will enter agreements as to how disputes are to be resolved. For example, they may agree to comply with the judgements of certain arbitration agencies. The separation of arbitration and enforcement significantly reduces the risk of conflict and it is in the long-term interest of protective agencies to respect the decisions made by arbitration agencies.

These agreements between different agencies, pace Nozick, do not however imply that we are dealing with a situation in which '[t]hough different agencies operate, there is one unified federal judicial system of which they are all components' (p. 16). Instead, there can be different arbitration agencies and different protective agencies which compete with each other. There can still be large differences between the agencies. Different agencies can enforce different rules, provide different services, charge different fees, entertain different customer bases, function according to different organizational principles, and can vary in various other ways. There is no particularly strong reason why we have to end up with a dominant protective agency, a single provider that has a de facto monopoly. Thus, it is still a possibility that anarchy is a feasible and superior alternative.

Both the transition from the dominant agency to the ultraminimal state and the transition therefrom to the minimal state have been criticized. On the one hand, Nozick's appeal to procedural rights to justify prohibiting independents from enforcing their rights has been claimed to be problematic. Some critics have objected that there are no such things as procedural rights. Barnett, for example, argues against procedural rights, noting that the legitimacy of self-defence is a question of fact. If someone's rights were infringed, then that person may legitimately defend himself. The question is whether rights were infringed and not what the epistemic state of the agent is or what procedures were used in assessing guilt. 'The rights of the parties are governed by the objective fact situation. The problem is to discern what the objective facts are, or, in other words, to make our subjective understanding of the facts conform to the objective facts themselves' (Barnett: 1977, p. 17). Determining who is right and who is wrong is a practical matter and not an issue of procedural rights.

Paul criticizes the idea that there are procedural rights by pointing to the infinitely regressive character of such rights. If one has a procedural right to the effect that one is to be judged according to fair and reliable procedures, then the question arises whether one has a procedural right to the effect that the assessment of the procedure be fair and reliable. That is, if we have a right regarding the procedure used to establish whether we are guilty or not, then it would seem that we should also have a right regarding the second-order procedure that is used to establish whether the first-order procedure used to establish whether we are guilty or not is fair and reliable and so on ad infinitum. We end up in a situation in which '[e]ach rights violation is potentially encumbered with an infinite set of decision procedures' (Paul: 1981, p. 73).

On the other hand, it has been argued that prohibiting independents from enforcing their own rights cannot be justified even if compensation is granted, given that rights are side constraints. Mack has argued that the compensation principle, which is crucial to Nozick's argument against the anarchist, is in conflict with Nozick's anti-consequentialist position. This principle is in danger of undermining the moral boundaries that give rise to side constraints. If consistently implemented, the compensation principle would allow for various forms of intervention that would be deemed unacceptable by Nozick.

The compensation principle ensures that we end up with an outcome-oriented conception of rights, according to which 'a boundary specifies a level of well-being and the permissibility of others' actions depends upon the effect of those actions upon the subject's wellbeing. . . . This shift to an outcome oriented conception of rights should make it difficult for Nozick to sustain his anti-paternalism' (Mack: 1981, p. 187). As long as a paternalistic intervention does not have a negative effect on the well-being of a subject, that subject has no cause for complaint. The permissibility of such intervention will depend on how it affects well-being and not on whether it involves coercion. This outcome-oriented conception is to be contrasted with a strictly deontic account of rights, according to which 'a boundary is a frontier which others do wrong to cross and accompanying benefits do not right such wrongs' (Mack: 1981, p. 187).

Nozick thus faces a dilemma. Either he retains his compensation principle, in which case he can no longer rule out paternalistic interventions that do not move the subject to a lower indifference curve. Or he sticks to the strictly deontic account that seems to be much more in line with his Kantian foundations, in which case he will have to give up the compensation principle. Giving up the compensation principle would require him to recant the claim that the dominant protective agency can legitimately prohibit independents from enforcing their rights as long as adequate compensation is given to them. This would undermine a key step in the derivation of the minimal state.

Moreover, the fact that the ultraminimal state has to provide compensation for prohibiting independents casts doubt on Nozick's claim that the minimal state can arise without violating any rights. Prima facie, it seems that compensation is only due if a wrong has been done. 'The disadvantage to independents resulting from the monopoly of force is morally wrong. It is for this reason that the independents deserve compensation' (Holmes: 1981, p. 61). This suggests that it is wrong to prohibit independents from enforcing their rights, that prohibition is illegitimate and involves the violation of a right, namely the right of self-defence. Accordingly, it turns out that the process by which the minimal state arises does involve morally illegitimate steps after all, even if the wrongs that have been done are compensated for.

Finally, the explanatory relevance of Nozick's hypothetical story has been questioned. While it is conceivable that a minimal state could have arisen in the way depicted by Nozick, it is not clear why this should be of any significance since no actual state has arisen in this way. As Miller notes, 'to say of a state that it *could* have arisen by such means is actually to say very little' (Miller: 2002, p. 19). Moreover, if what we are concerned with is the mere possibility of a legitimate state, it would seem to be sufficient to appeal to the possibility of a state coming into existence as a result of explicit consent since this would not violate any rights. Explicit consent would also do more in the way of justifying the state than an invisible-hand account since it would show that those setting up the state consider it as having positive value. An invisible-hand explanation does not have this virtue since it is compatible with its being the case that the emergence of the state is deemed to be a deterioration since 'it does not follow from the fact that people individually have reason to choose to sign up with the largest agency in their geographic region that collectively they have reason to applaud its emergence as a dominant agency' (Miller: 2002, p. 21). Thus, it seems that a hypothetical account has less justificatory strength than a historical account, and that, even though an invisible-hand explanation has certain explanatory virtues since it can take the form of a fundamental explanation that explains the political realm in non-political terms, it has less justificatory strength than an explicit consent explanation.

More than the minimal state?

Nozick's entitlement theory and his critique of patterned conceptions of justice have had a significant impact on political philosophy. All three aspects of the entitlement theory, namely the principles of justice in acquisition, transfer and rectification, have been criticized on numerous occasions.

To begin with, many people have pointed out the lack of an account of original acquisition. Without a theory of acquisition, the entitlement theory would break down. 'Before capitalist acts between consenting adults can take place in an orderly way, there must be solitary capitalist acts. Acquisition precedes transfer' (O'Neill: 1981, p. 320). Nozick raises a number of forceful objections against

Locke's theory of appropriation, which states that property can be acquired by mixing one's labour with something that is unowned. However, he does not put forward
a positive theory to replace the one proposed by Locke.
Instead, he simply gives a revised version of the Lockean
proviso. The modified proviso replaces the condition that
there be enough and as good left for others with the condition that no one be made worse off by the appropriation
than they would have been had the resource remained
unowned.

This confronts Nozick with a dilemma. Either compliance
with the proviso is seen as a necessary condition on justified acquisition, in which case we lack a theory of appropriation since we have only been given one necessary
condition and no sufficient conditions. Or compliance
with the proviso amounts to a sufficient condition insofar
as an act of appropriation can be justified simply in virtue
of not violating the proviso, in which case Nozick's theory
would not be very plausible. Taking compliance with the
proviso to be a sufficient condition would make any appropriation of unowned resources justified, unless it were to
clash with the Nozickian proviso. However, not making
other people worse off does not appear to be sufficient to
give rise to property rights. In particular, it does not seem
sufficient to establish the absolute property rights over
particular things that Nozick needs for his entitlement
theory. There seems to be a need for something more to
give rise to a right, to a claim on other people.

Moreover, the proviso has been criticized by a number of
people, most notably by G. A. Cohen. Cohen claims that
Nozick does not provide any arguments for taking the
situation in which the object remains unowned as the baseline for assessing appropriations. Instead, he suggests that
different schemes of appropriation should be considered.

That is, we should consider whether anyone will be worse off by the actual appropriation relative to other schemes of appropriation. If person X appropriates resource R, we should not only assess whether Y is worse off as a result of the appropriation than Y would have been had R remained unowned, but also assess whether Y is worse off than Y would have been had Y appropriated R or had X and Y jointly appropriated R. Nozick has not given us any arguments for accepting the baseline that he has picked and the one he has chosen may well turn out to be too weak.

In response, Mack has argued that Nozick does not consider the proviso as being a sufficient condition for an appropriation to be just, but only as a necessary condition. 'The fact that a set of holdings satisfies the proviso is not itself the primary vindication of those holdings; rather, this fact rebuts a particular challenge against presumptively justified holdings' (Mack: 2002, p. 100). Whether an appropriation is just is determined by the principles of justice in acquisition. These principles specify the procedures by means of which unowned resources can be appropriated. The performance of the relevant kinds of actions is sufficient for an appropriation to be justified, as long as it does not violate the proviso. Accordingly, it is the principles of justice in acquisition that are doing the justificatory work. Compliance with the proviso does not confer justification on an appropriation. It is not the case that an appropriation is justified because it complies with the proviso. Rather, the justification results from the process of appropriation.

Given this understanding of the role of the proviso, it becomes possible to deal with Cohen's challenge that Nozick's baseline ignores alternative schemes of appropriation. Mack points out that Cohen's critique is based on 'a moral equivalence between what has arisen and what

might have arisen. . . . Now this proposition about what
matters could, in some final analysis, be correct. What is
extraordinary, however, is that a critique of a historical
entitlement doctrine should take *as a premise* the proposition that the history of a set of holdings does not count'
(Mack: 2002, p. 102). Cohen's invocation of alternative
scenarios of appropriation assumes that there is nothing
about the actual scenario that gives rise to special claims,
nothing that privileges the actual appropriation over
counterfactual appropriations. An actual appropriation is
simply treated as being on a par with a counterfactual
appropriation. This, however, is inappropriate in the context of the entitlement theory since the principles of
justice in acquisition specify how rights arise out of the
performance of certain actions. Appropriators have a
claim in virtue of what they have done. For these claims to
arise, the actions obviously have to be performed in the
actual world. This implies that an appropriation in a counterfactual scenario does not give rise to any claims. It is
the actual historical processes that give rise to property
rights and that confer justification upon appropriations,
making counterfactual appropriations irrelevant.

Accordingly, Nozick should not be understood as treating compliance with the proviso as a sufficient condition.
Instead, an appropriation is justified if it takes place by
means of procedures specified by the principles of justice
in acquisition. Unfortunately, Nozick does not specify what
these principles are. Apart from the proviso, he does not
specify any necessary or sufficient conditions. This means
that he does not give us a theory of appropriation, but
only an outline of such a theory. This is problematic since
acquisition lies at the foundation of the entitlement theory.
While Nozick does not provide us with a worked-out theory

of original acquisition, it should be taken into consideration that he is in the same boat as pretty much everyone else. 'We should note that it is not only persons favoring *private* property who need a theory of how property rights legitimately originate' (p. 178). Every political philosophy and every account of justice in holdings needs a theory of property rights and a theory of original acquisition and no one has given a plausible account yet. While Nozick's view faces problems, there is a significant lack of better alternatives.

A different kind of criticism focusing on the proviso has been raised by Lyons and Waldron. They question whether the Nozickian proviso can be properly integrated into Nozick's rights-based moral framework, given that it seems to be introducing non-deontic considerations. 'The underlying idea is that property arrangements must accommodate the basic needs and interests (Nozick would probably say the rights) of others' (Lyons: 1981, p. 368). Similarly, Waldron argues that Nozick's 'theory begins with the assumption that the formation and justification of property entitlements must be responsive to concerns about well-being that are not embodied in property rights' (Waldron: 2005, p. 100). Accordingly, it seems that property rights are no longer fundamental but are subordinated to considerations regarding welfare. This is at odds with Nozick's deontological framework and threatens to undermine the purely procedural character of the entitlement theory.

Nozick is aware of these difficulties and tries to circumvent them by arguing that the proviso is not an end-state principle since 'it focuses on a particular way that appropriative actions affect others, and not on the structure of the situation that results' (p. 181). Accordingly, there can be structurally identical distributions that differ in whether they involve violations of the proviso. This can happen as long as the counterfactuals concerning these distributions differ. In particular, this happens if in one distribution some individuals would have been better off than they actually are had a particular resource remained unowned, while the corresponding counterfactual does not hold for the other distribution even though these distributions have the same structure. Thus, we can see that what matters for the proviso is not the structure of the resulting distribution but the effect of the appropriation, whereby this effect is assessed by comparing the actual scenario with the counterfactual scenario that would have obtained had the resource remained unowned.

In addition, we can see that satisfying the proviso is a matter of not harming others, rather than of accommodating their needs and interests. The proviso does not specify any positive rights that others have, but instead amounts to a condition that others are not to be harmed by an appropriation. Put differently, it is neither the case that people have a right to a particular level of welfare that has to be guaranteed, nor that there are basic interests and needs that have to be met. The restriction on appropriation is essentially a no-harm condition and is thereby simply an instance of the general condition that our actions are not to result in harm to other people. In the same way that we are not to harm other people by killing or injuring them, we are not to harm them by appropriative acts that make them worse off than they would have been had the resource remained unowned, i.e. by appropriative acts that fail to satisfy the proviso.

We saw in the previous chapter that the principles of justice in transfer form a crucial aspect of the entitlement theory. These principles specify which transfers are justice-preserving and thereby determine how we can get from one set of holdings that is just to another set that is also just. Nozick's main argument in favour of a procedural account that treats all voluntary transfers (that do not violate the proviso) as being just was the Wilt Chamberlain example. This example is supposed to establish that it is not reasonable to reject the entitlement theory.

Nozick's claim that liberty upsets patterns has been criticized on the basis that individuals could choose to act in such a way as to not upset the pattern. In this case, no interference would be required. 'Nozick must concede that it is possible a pattern may remain reasonably stable even given voluntary transactions' (Wolff: 1991, p. 82). This objection is somewhat misplaced. Even if there would not be any need for significant interferences with the choices of individuals, it would still be the case that a large range of voluntary transfers would have to be prohibited, namely all those which would upset the pattern. While individuals in this imagined situation would not want to upset the pattern, the real point is that they could upset the pattern without doing any wrong. Put differently, Nozick allows that holdings can conform to patterns, but claims that justness is not to be based on any patterns. Thus, the crucial argument is not that liberty necessarily upsets patterns (though Nozick does think that it is likely that liberty upsets patterns, given that it would be practically impossible to co-ordinate the actions of a large number of individuals such as to maintain a pattern, cf. p. 163), but that it would be legitimate for people to upset the pattern. Nozick wants to argue that voluntary transfers are justice-preserving and that they can upset a pattern, which implies that justness is not a matter of conforming to any pattern. Accordingly, the justness is not based on the structure of the distribution, but on the procedures that give rise to the distribution.

It has been objected on a number of occasions that the Wilt Chamberlain example presupposes Nozick's understanding of rights, rather than establishing it. This would render the Wilt Chamberlain argument dialectically ineffective. Holdings are justly distributed under D1 and Nozick claims that D2 is also just since we arrive at it by means of voluntary transfers. The transition is effected by individuals voluntarily exchanging some of the holdings that they are entitled to under D1. This claim has been criticized since it presupposes that the individuals have full capitalist ownership rights over the resources they received under D1, i.e. that they can do whatever they want with their holdings. Nagel objects that Nozick 'erroneously interprets the notion of a patterned principle as specifying a distribution of *absolute entitlements* (like those he believes in) to the wealth or property distributed' (Nagel: 1981, p. 201; also cf. Cohen: 1995, p. 28).

Put differently, the criticism states that ownership rights do not necessarily imply an unrestricted right to transfer. 'Different conceptions of justice differ not only in how they would apportion society's holdings but in what rights individuals have over their holdings once they have been apportioned' (Ryan: 1981, p. 331). Nozick's example thus presupposes libertarian rights and in particular the right that one can do with one's holdings whatever one wants. Unless it can be shown that individuals have an unrestricted right to transfer the holdings that they have received under D1, it will not be the case that the transition to D2 is justice-preserving. 'The argument presupposes, so does not demonstrate, that it is wrong to interfere to restore disturbed patterns or end-states, and that such restorations are always redistributive and violate individuals' property rights. But it is just these property rights which have yet to be established'

(O'Neill: 1981, pp. 308–309). There is thus an urgent need for an argument that establishes full capitalist property rights. Nozick, however, does not provide any principles of appropriation that establish such property rights.

In response, one can note that it would at the very least be counter-intuitive to claim that all voluntary transfers that upset patterns, including seemingly harmless transfers such as gift-giving, are unjust. While Nozick does believe in full capitalist rights, his argument against patterned theories does not require such rights. It only requires that there be some kinds of transfers, such as gift-giving, that are justice-preserving in virtue of their procedural properties. Given that the correct procedure is followed, the outcome is just even if it upsets the pattern. The idea that some voluntary transfers are justice-preserving even if they upset a pattern has been accepted by some of Nozick's critics. For example, Wolff states: 'Despite the problems raised, however, we should acknowledge that we must permit at least *some* voluntary transfers, unless, as Nozick repeatedly reminds us, we wish to prohibit "gift-giving and other loving behaviour"' (Wolff: 1991, p. 88).

The significance of this concession, however, has not been fully appreciated. Wolff does not seem to be aware that this is to concede that patterned conceptions cannot be upheld. At least, no pure patterned theories can be upheld. There may still be room for patterns in specifying what makes the initial distribution just, but the specification of what makes ulterior distributions just will be in terms of the procedures that give rise to these distributions. In other words, conceding Nozick's point regarding voluntary transfers still leaves room for a patterned account of original acquisition, but it implies a commitment to a procedural account of justice in transfer. This does not mean that we automatically end up with Nozick's entitlement theory, but only that we have to accept some form of procedural rather than structural account of the principles of transfer. Which kinds of voluntary transfers are considered to be justice-preserving will then determine the precise nature of the procedural theory. Nozick believes that all voluntary transfers are justice-preserving. Other procedural accounts that only admit a restricted range of voluntary transfers are also possible and it seems that Wolff has such a restriction in mind.

Admitting that some voluntary transfers are justice-preserving implies that the resulting theory will no longer be a structural account. This means that a distribution cannot be judged to be just or unjust by simply considering the relative holdings of different individuals. Instead, one will have to look at how the distribution arose and assess whether the transfers leading to that distribution satisfied the procedural conditions. This also implies that pretty much any possible set of holdings, no matter how unequal, may turn out to be just as long as it has arisen in the correct manner and as long as it does not violate the proviso. For example, if the transfer of holdings through gifts is considered to be justice-preserving, then we can end up with a just distribution whereby one person controls most resources if these have been acquired as a result of gift-giving.

A further reply to the criticism that Nozick's argument presupposes full capitalist ownership rights has been given by Roderick Long. He questions whether the rights people have over the holdings they receive under D1 can still be called ownership rights, given the severity of the restrictions that pattern theorists must impose. If someone has received certain holdings but is not allowed to transfer or utilize them in any way that upsets the pattern, then it becomes dubious whether that person can be said to own those holdings (cf. Long: 2002).

Furthermore, we can note that these rights are extremely fleeting given that pattern theories generally fail to satisfy the addition and deletion conditions (cf. pp. 209–210). Thus, the 'property rights' accorded by pattern theories are highly restrictive and unstable, which makes it questionable whether they properly classify as ownership rights at all. These points are connected to the argument we gave in the previous chapter, showing that the Wilt Chamberlain argument establishes that pattern theories are partly self-defeating. This is because the restrictions on transfers required to maintain the pattern partly undermine the point of distributing in the first place. Thus the rights that people do have over their holdings under D1 seem so insignificant that it seems inappropriate to call them ownership rights and that it becomes questionable why they are valuable at all.

Independently of considerations regarding ownership, the Wilt Chamberlain example is intended to show that justice, as construed by the pattern theorist, is in conflict with liberty. Even if it were granted that critics are correct in pointing out that Nozick cannot make claims about redistribution being unjust since this would presuppose the entitlement theory, it would seem that this would not fully defuse the Wilt Chamberlain example. Redistributing to maintain the pattern would not be unjust if people were to have highly restricted 'ownership' rights over their holdings. Yet, the maintaining of a pattern would nonetheless be problematic due to infringements of liberty and interferences with people's lives. Nozick argues that upholding a pattern requires significant interferences in people's lives and requires the prohibition of many voluntary actions.

This is problematic independently of whether or not such restrictions and interferences classify as infringements of people's property rights.

In response to this line of argument, it has been pointed out by Cheyney Ryan that, even though pattern theorists have to impose restrictions on what people may do with their holdings, 'whether or not this lack of freedom constitutes an infringement on personal *liberty* depends on the rights we have over the holding in question' (Ryan: 1981, p. 330). Given Nozick's rights-based definition of liberty, it follows that there is no infringement of liberty in the absence of the infringement of rights. Nozick argues that people are only free to do those things they have a right to do. Accordingly, Nozick cannot uphold the claim that the maintaining of patterns involves the infringement of liberty unless he presupposes capitalist ownership rights. 'To prove that liberty upsets patterns, Nozick must undertake the burden of proving that people do have the right to make whatever transfers they wish. Liberty is no longer fundamental' (Wolff: 1991, p. 96). Put differently, a pattern theorist who adopts Nozick's rights-based definition of liberty can argue that patterns are not in conflict with liberty since we only have rights to transfer holdings in ways that do not upset the pattern. Since transfers that upset patterns are unjust, we are not free to perform such transfers. Consequently, the prohibition of these transfers will not constitute a restriction on liberty understood in this moralized sense.

If the rights-based definition of liberty is relinquished, a different problem arises. It will then be the case that the entitlement theory is also in conflict with liberty. This is because capitalist property rights can be seen as inhibiting freedom, given that they impose boundaries on what other people can do and restrict the range of alternatives open to individuals. Capitalist property rights reduce freedom by imposing constraints on what other people can do. 'Any given set of rights (such as private property rights) insures some freedoms (such as the freedom to exchange) but also thwarts others (the freedom of others to use property now privately owned)' (Ryan: 1981, p. 340).

This means that Nozick faces a dilemma. On the one hand, he can retain his rights-based definition of liberty, in which case questions of liberty cannot be settled unless questions of right have been settled. Accordingly, he will have to presuppose capitalist ownership rights in order to claim that the maintaining of a pattern infringes liberty. This, however, would imply that the Wilt Chamberlain example presupposes rather than establishes the entitlement theory. As a result, the argument would be dialectically ineffective since it would be begging the question against those who reject full capitalist ownership rights. On the other hand, he can give up the rights-based definition of liberty, in which case he would be justified in claiming that liberty upsets patterns, but his opponents would be equally correct in pointing out that liberty also upsets entitlements. Any theory of property that places restrictions on what people can do would be in conflict with liberty understood in this non-moralized sense. The best Nozick could then do is to try to argue that the entitlement theory gives us more freedom and places less restrictions on what can be done, or that the freedoms it gives us are more important and the restrictions less onerous than those resulting from patterned theories.

While the pattern theorist can consistently claim that maintaining a pattern does not restrict liberty, he must nonetheless impose significant restrictions on a range of intuitively unproblematic actions. While such a position is coherent, it is still counterintuitive since it imposes high costs on society by prohibiting a large number of mutually beneficial exchanges. These restrictions give rise to the self-defeating character of pattern theories that we have pointed to previously. Property matters according to pattern theorists because of its beneficial effects. However, it is not sufficient that people possess property for these effects to arise. Instead, they must be able to use it and exchange it and this they cannot do if the restrictions required for maintaining patterns are put in place.

Another prominent objection to Nozick's claim that liberty upsets patterns is that within a Rawlsian framework justice only applies to the basic structure of society, which implies that there is no commitment to constant redistribution and interference to maintain a pattern (cf. Pogge: 1989, p. 29; Kukathas and Pettit: 1990, pp. 89–90). Put differently, if what it takes for a society to be just is for its basic institutional structure to be just, then the divergence of a distribution of holdings from a pattern does not constitute an injustice that has to be prohibited or rectified. 'It is a mistake to focus attention on the varying relative positions of individuals and to require that every change, considered as a single transaction viewed in isolation, be in itself just. It is the arrangement of the basic structure which is to be judged, and judged from a general point of view' (Rawls: 1971, pp. 87–88; also cf. Rawls: 1977, p. 164).

Mack has responded to this objection by pointing out that 'for the pattern theorist, the justice of the basic structure and its activities still ultimately turns on that structure's propensity to bring about the pattern of holdings that is the ultimate justifying purpose of that basic structure' (Mack: 2002, p. 85). Unless the basic structure prohibits moving from D1 to D2 or requires that D2 be converted into a distribution D3 that is again in conformity with the pattern, it will not do its job of bringing about the desired pattern of holdings and will consequently turn out to be unjust.

Waldron provides a similar argument, noting that even though a Rawlsian is not committed to reallocating holdings in case they should diverge from the pattern since society will be governed by the basic structure, it is nonetheless the case that he will have to ask himself whether we can 'change the institutional structure (including the structure of property entitlements, if there are any) so as to render it more likely in the future that the normal operation of our economy will yield distributions [that conform more closely to the pattern]' (Waldron: 2005, p. 107). If it is possible to modify the institutional structure in such a way, for instance by prohibiting voluntary exchanges that upset the pattern or by requiring the reallocation of resources to restore the pattern, then this is something that justice requires. In other words, if we are concerned with the basic structure of society, then a patterned conception of justice does not tell us to intervene and reallocate resources to reinstate the pattern, but tells us to alter the basic structure. Intervention will consequently still be demanded by a patterned conception of justice but will now be directed at the basic structure rather than directly at the distribution of holdings.

A related objection is that pattern theorists do not require constant interference since 'they tend to advocate an approximation of the preferred pattern, the value of which is tempered by the value of liberty, and vice versa' (Hailwood: 1996, p. 33; also cf. Wolff: 1991, pp. 88–90). Pattern theories are usually understood as involving the redistribution of holdings according to predictable and publicly known rules, by means of some form of progressive taxation that is combined with welfare benefits, rather than the strict and rigid implementation of a pattern. While such a taxation scheme interferes with liberty to some extent, it will not amount to the constant and intrusive interference with people's lives that Nozick depicts.

It is true that, all things considered, a pattern theorist need not be committed to such extensive interference since other considerations, such as the rule of law, can function as mitigating factors. Nonetheless, such extensive interference is required as far as justice is concerned and this surely speaks against a patterned theory of justice. In other words, the fact that the counter-intuitive consequences of a theory of justice are mitigated by other components of a political philosophy does not change the fact that the theory of justice has highly counter-intuitive consequences. It seems that a theory of justice should be able to stand on its own. It should not be something that is defective and that needs to be supplemented to be rendered acceptable.

Moreover, this implies that such pattern theorists have to make trade-offs and cannot be fully committed to distributive justice. They will have to balance justice against other considerations and can at best approximate what they would consider to be a just distribution. This is something an entitlement theorist does not have to do. Nozick's political philosophy does not consist of different components that conflict and have to be weighed up against each other. As a result, Nozick can be unreservedly committed to liberty, justice and the rule of law. The different components of his theory are fully compatible and no trade-offs need to be made.

A further criticism of the Wilt Chamberlain example is that Nozick ignores significant negative effects on third parties that result from moving from D1 to D2. Nozick claims that third parties are unaffected by the change and have no cause for complaint because their shares remain the same. This view is criticized by Cohen. He argues that 'a person's effective share depends on what he can do with what he has, and that depends not only on how much he has but on what others have and on how what others have is distributed' (Cohen: 1995, pp. 26–27). Thus, while the shares of third parties remain the same, Cohen wants to say that an injustice can arise in the change from D1 to D2 since the way holdings are distributed will have effects on third parties and will determine what can be done with those shares. Certain individuals, such as Wilt Chamberlain, will have access to significant resources under D2 and can use them in ways that are detrimental to third parties. In other words, Cohen argues that changes in the distribution of resources can lead to changes in the power relations that negatively affect third parties, thereby giving rise to injustice.

Nozick's response to this claim is that while it is indeed true that Wilt Chamberlain has a great deal of resources under D2 and is consequently in a position to do things that others were not able to do individually under D1, it was nonetheless the case that others could jointly do those very same things under D1 (cf. p. 162, footnote). There is thus an important sense in which effective shares of third parties remain the same. No new powers have emerged that were not already implicitly contained in the previous distribution. The range of things that could be done under D1 is the same as that which obtains under D2. All that has changed is which individuals or groups of individuals can do these things. Accordingly, there is no cause for complaint by third parties. Moreover, Nozick notes that the objection focusing on effects on third parties does not apply to 'distributions of ultimate intrinsic noninstrumental goods (pure utility experiences, so to speak) that are transferable' (p. 162, footnote). The transfer of such noninstrumental goods cannot affect the effective shares of third parties, which means that voluntary exchanges are justice-preserving at least for these goods.

In addition to the Wilt Chamberlain example, Nozick put forward an argument to the effect that income taxation constitutes a violation of self-ownership and that it is on a par with forced labour. According to patterned accounts of justice, the holdings that are allocated to individuals are specified by some pattern. The pattern determines how the social product is to be distributed among different people and what share of the product is due to particular people. Patterned theories thereby give individuals a claim on the social product, which means that they have a claim on the activities and products of other people. This then makes them part owners in other people. Accordingly, patterned theories are in conflict with self-ownership. They are incompatible with the idea that 'every person is morally entitled to full private property in his own person and powers. This means that each person has an extensive set of moral rights . . . over the use and fruits of his body and capacities' (Cohen: 1995, p. 117).

Cohen claims that this argument based on the self-ownership thesis is the most fundamental argument in favour of libertarianism. '[T]he primary commitment of [Nozick's] philosophy is not to liberty but to the thesis of self-ownership. . . . "Libertarianism" affirms not freedom as such, but freedom of a certain type, whose shape is delineated by the thesis of self-ownership' (Cohen: 1995, p. 67). Wolff makes a similar claim, arguing that the 'right to liberty is, on this view, purely formal. It is, in essence, merely the right to do what you have a right to do' (Wolff: 1991, p. 96). The Wilt Chamberlain example tries to draw a connection between freedom and justice, but claims about freedom depend on rights, given the rights-based definition of freedom. These rights are the rights of self-ownership and it is they that determine what counts as an infringement of liberty. Accordingly, the Wilt Chamberlain argument is effective only to the extent to which it is based on the self-ownership thesis, which implies that no independent argument from freedom against patterned accounts is to be found.

Cohen grants that Nozick is correct in pointing out that taxation of earnings from labour amounts to instituting partial ownership in other people. Self-ownership is not 'consistent with a directive that, whenever I use [my talents] for my own benefit, I must, to a stated extent, use them to benefit others too: that is the essence of redistributive income taxation. I do not (fully) own myself if I am required to give others (part of) what I earn by applying my powers' (Cohen: 1995, p. 216). Accordingly, those in favour of redistributive income taxation need to reject the self-ownership thesis.

Though Cohen accepts that he cannot refute the self-ownership thesis, he claims to be able to show that the denial of it is relatively unproblematic. He attempts to do this by establishing that the intuitive support for self-ownership actually derives from other principles that are separable from self-ownership and that can be preserved even when the self-ownership thesis is rejected. In particular, he claims that the appeal of self-ownership derives from conflating the idea of being a self-owner with the ideas of (i) not being a slave, (ii) possessing autonomy and (iii) not being used merely as a means (cf. Cohen: 1995, p. 230). While all these three features are highly important, Cohen claims that they are separable from self-ownership and can therefore be retained even when the self-ownership thesis is denied.

A characteristic feature of the entitlement theory that is not shared by many other conceptions is that it implies a commitment to there being entitlements to particular things. People are entitled to particular things that they have appropriated, created or received. It is not just that they are entitled to a particular quantity of goods or to a particular amount of holdings, but that they have entitlements to particular objects.

Davis provides an interesting critique of this aspect of the entitlement theory, arguing that it causes problems for the definition of a just distribution as well as for the principles of rectification (cf. Davis: 1981). His critique appeals to cases that involve the destruction of objects that have been illegitimately acquired. Davis argues that a situation in which someone steals certain things and then destroys them satisfies Nozick's definition of justice since the holdings of everyone have been arrived at in a just manner. In particular, the thief does not have any holdings that have been unjustly acquired since all the stolen goods were destroyed. Accordingly, Nozick's definition needs to be amended. In particular, it turns out that Nozick's claim that a distribution is just if everyone's holdings have been justly acquired is problematic and cannot deal with the cases invoked by Davis.

While this characterization of the entitlement theory is problematic, Nozick's recursive definition of a just distribution that is specified in terms of the three sets of principles of the entitlement theory can adequately handle these cases. The reason for the inadequacy of the former definition is that it only looks at the holdings people do have and not the holdings that people do not have. This oversight is rectified by the latter definition since it is concerned with the manner in which we move from one set of holdings to another, whereby this includes processes by which people divest themselves of properties. Thus, the set of holdings resulting from the destruction of unjustly acquired objects is unjust since some of the steps leading to it contravene the principles of justice in transfer.

While Nozick's recursive definition can handle the cases described by Davis, the principle of rectification lacks the resources to deal with such cases. That is, cases involving the destruction of illegitimately acquired property give rise to problems for the principle of rectification. This is because the objects to which people were entitled have been destroyed and consequently cannot be returned to their rightful owners. There is nothing for the principles of rectification to do in such cases. Davis suggests that Nozick can overcome this difficulty by appealing to the compensation principle. This, however, will imply that we no longer have a pure entitlement theory. We no longer look at the particular objects to which people are entitled but rather assess the utility that they derive from the objects and compensate them if they have been wronged, not by returning the particular objects to which they are entitled, but by ensuring that they end up on the same indifference curve. The compensation principle thereby introduces a utility criterion into the principles of rectification of the entitlement theory that seems to be at odds with the rights-based account of justice.

A common objection against Nozick's project is that the entitlement theory is largely irrelevant since we lack the requisite historical and counterfactual information to ascertain which set of holdings would be just. Accordingly, we are unable to implement the principle of rectification, which means that we will not be able to rectify past injustices and bring about a just distribution. While the entitlement theory might be an interesting account of how things should work under ideal conditions, it does not seem to be applicable to the real world.

Schmidtz has pointed out that '[v]oluntary transfer cannot cleanse a tainted title of original sin, but any injustice in the result will have been preexisting, not created by the transfer. We are fated to live in a world of background injustice. . . . Still, Nozick thinks, it remains possible for moral agents, living ordinary lives, to abide by his principle of just transfer and, to that extent, to have clean hands' (Schmidtz: 2005, pp. 160–161). Thus, the entitlement theory and the principles of justice in transfer in particular are still of importance, even if it is not possible in practice to comprehensively apply this theory to bring about a just set of holdings. In other words, the principles of just transfer tell us how we can avoid making things worse, allowing those who abide by these principles to live with a clear conscience. That is, if we follow the entitlement theory as far as our epistemic situation allows, then we know at a minimum that we are not creating further injustices. In addition, we can note that there are cases where no injustices have occurred that could compromise the applicability of the entitlement theory, as happens for instance when we are dealing with certain cases of intellectual property rights (cf. pp. 181–182). Problems regarding the rectification of past injustices do not matter when it comes to questions concerning newly created holdings. With respect to these holdings at least, the entitlement theory can be followed comprehensively in practice.

Problems with the meta-utopia

Nozick's discussion of utopia has unfortunately been much neglected. It has not generated a great deal of discussion and has accordingly only been subjected to a small number of criticisms, most of which have focused on practical concerns regarding the applicability of the framework to the actual world.

One criticism that has been raised on several occasions is that market mechanisms will lead to a situation in which we end up with a dominant culture. 'Could a community that wanted a lot of redistribution survive the departure of the wealthy members whose moral principles are weaker than their desire for wealth? . . . [C]ould a community maintain its dedication to an austere life of virtue if it were surrounded by the flashy temptations of American capitalism?' (Singer: 1981, p. 38). Nozick's description of the framework suggests that we end up with an inspiring pluralistic society consisting of a large number of diverse associations in which different people pursue their own utopian visions. Nozick's critics, however, maintain that the pressure of the market will lead to the emergence of a dominant culture, namely a vulgar, consumption-oriented capitalist culture. There is then seen to be a need for political action to ensure that certain ways of life will not die out. This will require an extensive state that raises taxes to subsidize such endangered communities and that shields them from the competitive pressure of the market.

Nozick's reply would probably be that freedom comes with responsibility, that people have to pay the price of their choices and that they should not impose their preferences on others. Of course, some forms of life may die out. People will decide that living in a certain way is too costly, that it is not worth it. The framework for utopia is a good mechanism for finding out the real price of a life-style. It allows us to identify what its costs and benefits are and then lets people decide whether they are willing to pay this price. This seems much better than imposing a life-style on people who or not willing to pay its price or than subsidizing the life-style of a particular group at the expense of a large number of people who do not benefit from it and do not agree with it.

Moreover, Nozick would be likely to respond that there is going to be a sufficient degree of pluralism. After all, one of his arguments for the meta-utopia is that people are so diverse that there is no single way of living that is best for all of them. People 'differ in temperament, interests, intellectual ability, aspirations, natural bent, spiritual quests, and the kind of life they whish to lead. They diverge in the values they have and have different weightings for the values they share' (pp. 309–310). Within the framework this diversity among people will give rise to a plurality of diverse associations since individuals will have the freedom to experiment, to create, exit and join non-coercive associations. Finally, even if a dominant culture were to emerge, this would not be a problem as long as it is not enforced or imposed against people's will. What is the problem if everyone should decide to live similar life-styles regulated by similar rules? It is not evident that there is a problem since it is their choice. They have to decide how to live their lives.

To this it can be objected that 'Nozick's vision of utopia fails to deal with the fundamental Marxist objection to classical liberalism: people make choices, but they do so under given historical circumstances which influence their choices. We do not enable people to govern their lives by giving them a "free" choice within these limits while refusing to do anything about the contexts in which these choices are made' (Singer: 1981, pp. 38–39). But if voluntary choices are not enough, then what is it that should be done? Imposing a certain way of life on individuals against their will is unlikely to achieve much good. Moreover, it is not clear why we should presume that those doing the imposing are not equally subject to the corrupting influences. Yet, to some extent Nozick does engage with this criticism. He wants to make sure that people are adequately informed of the various possibilities that are available, and that they not remain members of their associations ignorant of the alternatives. This applies in particular to children. While Nozick is aware of the difficulties, he does not provide any answers to them.

While most objections are concerned with practical problems regarding the implementation of the framework for utopia, Simon Hailwood has raised a number of criticisms focusing on the theoretical aspects of the framework. In particular, he questions whether Nozick is able to provide an account of the framework for utopia that does not appeal to any moral considerations and consequently provides independent support for the minimal state. Hailwood thinks that Nozick smuggles in various moral premises in developing and defending the meta-utopia. On the one hand, Nozick seems to presuppose that we should be neutral between different conceptions of the good. This neutrality is important since he rules out imperialistic utopian conceptions because they fail to be neutral. Similarly, Mack has claimed that Nozick's argument only applies to utopians 'whose ideal does not include the use of coercion against others as an end valuable in itself or as a necessary prelude to utopia. In this respect the argument is not independent of the voluntarism central to natural rights theory' (Mack: 1975, p. 10).

On the other hand, Nozick requires a criterion for best-ness given that he analyses utopia as the best possible world. The requisite criterion seems to be a moral criterion. Not only is it a moral criterion, but it appears that Nozick has to appeal to broadly consequentialist considerations to specify which world is the best of all possible worlds. With-out this consequentialist axiology, Nozick would lack a value-scale that would allow him to give a non-vacuous account of the framework of utopia. This gives rise to the question as to whether this argument is compatible with the deontological picture defended in the rest of the book. That is, Nozick's analysis suggests a consequentialist crite-rion of bestness understood in terms of preference satis-faction that is 'at odds with the anti consequentialism of the rest of *Anarchy, State, and Utopia*' (Hailwood: 1996, p. 77).

4

Relevance

There is no doubt that Nozick's work has had and will continue to have a significant impact on political philosophy. *Anarchy, State, and Utopia* is a fascinating book that is full of interesting ideas, compelling examples, thought-provoking suggestions, trenchant criticisms and powerful arguments. It is not a dogmatic statement of a doctrine, but the unfolding of a philosophical position by one of the greatest philosophers of the twentieth century. The central messages of the book remain highly relevant and important, even if in most cases there is still a great deal of work to be done in order to arrive at a satisfactory position.

This chapter attempts to give an assessment of what is still viable within the Nozickian project. It tries to set out what lines of research are still open, which aspects of his work have been unjustly neglected and ignored and what parts of this project have survived the criticisms. In short, this chapter gives an account of the legacy of Robert Nozick. While many of Nozick's critiques of other positions and arguments are insightful and worth keeping in mind, in this chapter we will mainly focus on some of the positive arguments, assumptions and approaches that Nozick makes use of in *Anarchy, State, and Utopia*.

Rights-based libertarianism

Nozick's work reinvigorated rights-based libertarianism, showing that this can be a highly fruitful research agenda. Rights-based approaches were prominent in the early modern period, in particular within the context of theistic moral frameworks where moral laws were considered to be divinely ordained. However, they had become neglected in recent times and were instead replaced by consequential-ist accounts that primarily appeal to economic arguments. 'With the exception of Robert Nozick, no major theorist in the Anglo-Saxon world for almost a century has based his work on the concept of a right' (Tuck: 1979, p. 1).

A distinctive feature of Nozick's project is that he advocates the minimal state on the basis of considerations regarding rights. Nozick does not follow the majority of contemporary libertarians and classical liberals in giving an economic, efficiency-based argument for libertarianism that depends on implicit or explicit utilitarian presupposi-tions. Instead, he places great importance on individual rights and the need to respect the separateness and dignity of persons. He suggests that we should consider rights as side constraints, thereby avoiding a utilitarianism of rights. All this is done in a non-theistically based framework since he provides a natural rights understanding of morality that does not depend on theistic premises. Accordingly, his project can be considered as a modernized, agnostic or atheistic version of the Lockean project.

Rights-based libertarianism has several advantages that are nicely exhibited by Nozick's arguments. To begin with, a rights-based approach is appealing because of the role it accords to the dignity of human beings. It thereby gives a central role to the value of individuals. Individuals are not

merely treated as loci of utilities but as inviolable beings
that have intrinsic worth. The rights-based approach takes
the dignity of individuals as the starting point and then
assesses what rights follow therefrom and what kinds of
political systems are compatible with these rights. A necessary condition on the legitimacy of a political system is that
it respects the dignity of individuals. Respecting rights is
the sine qua non of any mode of social organization.

By appealing to rights, we can defend a normative system
that is not dependent on problematic utilitarian assumptions or presuppositions. While rights-based approaches
face problems when it comes to providing a foundation for
individual rights, these problems seem less troublesome
than the difficulties faced by utilitarians. Nozick's arguments against utilitarianism and other consequentialist
theories are quite decisive, leaving rights-based approaches
as the best candidates for normative theories that wish to
take seriously the inviolability and separateness of persons.

Rights-based libertarianism does not make the justification (or lack thereof) of the state contingent on empirical
matters of facts. The legitimacy of the state does not boil
down to a question of efficiency and is therefore not an
empirical question. Instead, it can be dealt with in an a
priori manner. We can identify rights and assess what social
arrangements are compatible with these rights, without
appealing to empirical contingencies. This gives us a clear-
cut account of which actions are right and wrong, permitted and forbidden. It thus allows us to give a clear-cut
answer as to whether the state is legitimate at all and what
functions it may legitimately perform. Of course, we still
need to look at empirical matters of fact to assess whether
any particular state does comply with these constraints, in
particular whether the state has arisen in an appropriate

way. The normative question, however, can be settled independently of these empirical matters and can be given a
clear-cut answer.

A further advantage is that rights-based arguments provide a more robust foundation for libertarianism. Such
arguments for libertarianism cannot be avoided by simply
responding that economic efficiency can be sacrificed for
some other good, such as equality. Rights constitute the
side constraints within which various values play a role.
Such values, however, cannot override the constraints
deriving from individual rights and accordingly cannot
justify the transgression of these moral boundaries. In
other words, rights are prior to other values. This implies
that a rights-based version of libertarianism is resistant to
the invocation of various values. This, however, is not the
case when giving an efficiency-based argument for the
minimal state.

In short, adopting a rights-based approach allows us to
give a more plausible, more appealing and more robust
argument in favour of libertarianism that is not contingent
on empirical facts and that cannot easily be avoided by
invoking other values.

Any such understanding of libertarianism faces the problem of finding an adequate foundation for these negative
rights that are considered as side constraints if one is to
avoid Nagel's charge of advocating libertarianism without
foundations. As discussed previously, *Anarchy, State, and
Utopia* is not intended as a foundational project. Rather, it
is supposed to show what conclusions can be derived from
the intuitively plausible starting point that individuals do
have rights. Nonetheless, Nozick's discussion of rights is
highly relevant for other theorists attempting to provide a
rights-based account. This applies to the moral arguments
that Nozick invokes in favour of a rights-based approach,

as well as to the problems he identifies which rights-based theories need to address.

Nozick makes a convincing case for treating rights as side constraints. Rights are supposed to place limits on actions. They are supposed to reflect moral boundaries that should not be crossed. However, unless rights are treated as side constraints, they are unable to fulfil this role since it will be legitimate to violate rights and to transgress moral boundaries as long as this minimizes the overall level of rights violations. This utilitarianism of rights is unacceptable and does not sufficiently respect the inviolability of persons. The same considerations that made us reject utilitarianism and appeal to rights speak against allowing a utilitarianism of rights. Accordingly, rights ought not to be included in the end that is to be achieved. Rather, they should be understood as side constraints on actions that are not to be transgressed. They constrain the way in which ends are to be achieved, rather than featuring in the end that is to be achieved.

Moreover, Nozick's other discussions of ethics, in particular in *Philosophical Explanations*, are helpful in understanding what role rights can play in an ethical theory and how a foundation of them might be provided. In particular, his distinction between 'ethical-pull' and 'ethical-push' is of importance for ethical theories in general and rights-based accounts in particular. Ethical constraints can have two sources, namely the agent and the one acted upon. Ethical-pull is the normative force that specifies how a person is to be treated by others in virtue of the moral status of that person. The nature of the person acted upon imposes constraints on how he should be treated. Ethical-push, on the contrary, is the normative force that specifies how an agent should treat other people in virtue of the moral status that the agent himself possesses. The nature of the agent imposes constraints upon how he should act. In particular, he should act in such a way as is appropriate for the kind of person he is. That is, normative considerations derive both from the nature of the agent doing the acting and the nature of the person who is acted upon. These considerations seem to favour a rights-based moral theory, insofar as it adequately accounts for the ethical-pull deriving from the dignity of persons. The ethical-pull is represented in the moral theory in the form of rights that constitute side constraints on actions.

Furthermore, the relation between the different levels of ethics outlined in *The Examined Life* and in *Invariances*, is helpful for rights-based approaches. Nozick specifies different layers of a moral system, whereby the goals at higher levels are to be achieved without violating the constraints and undermining the goals of the lower levels. He starts with (i) an ethic of respect, followed by (ii) an ethic of responsiveness, (iii) an ethic of care and finally (iv) an ethic of light. This kind of layered approach allows us to integrate rights-based deontological considerations into a broader ethical system. The core area of ethics, which forms the most fundamental layer, is characterized by rights and is based on deontological considerations. The other levels have different sources and give rise to different moral structures. As regards political philosophy, the main focus will be on the core of ethics since only rights bring with them correlative duties that are enforceable and accordingly belong into the political realm.

Taking anarchism seriously

Nozick differs from many contemporary political philosophers due to the fact that he takes anarchism seriously.

This difference arises as a result of his strong emphasis on individual rights. Given these rights, it becomes questionable whether there is any room for a legitimate state. The strict understanding of rights and the importance accorded to voluntary consent seem to preclude the possibility of a legitimate state that is not based on explicit consent. Nozick recognizes this and consequently takes seriously the anarchist's challenge. As a result, he inquires as to how, if at all, a legitimate state can arise in the absence of explicit consent.

The question whether and under which conditions a legitimate state can arise is an important foundational question. Yet, this question is often ignored. Most political theorizing takes place on the implicit assumption that states can be legitimate, that they should exist and that they should perform various functions. The question then is simply seen to be what the state should do and how it should do it, rather than whether there should be a state at all. This implicit assumption is often not questioned. Instead, the existence and justification of the state is simply taken for granted. Nozick points out that this implicit assumption is quite a weighty assumption and that there is a serious question at issue here that ought to be addressed.

Not only is there an implicit assumption that states can be and often are legitimate, but there is also an implicit assumption that the state is necessary for achieving a desirable social condition. Many people simply assume that we need a state. The idea that a peaceful prospering cooperative society could be possible in the absence of a state is seen as anathema. The state is considered to be a necessity and only few people treat it is a necessary evil. The absence of a state is generally equated with disorder and chaos. Hobbes's claim that life would be nasty, brutish and short if there were no state to provide and enforce laws is widely accepted without being supported by arguments.

Nozick's direct engagement with the anarchist's challenge brings out these implicit assumptions about the legitimacy and necessity of a state. Accordingly, we can identify two important questions that need to be addressed. On the one hand, there is the question regarding the normative status of the state, namely whether the existence of a state can be justified at all. On the other, there is the empirical/ descriptive question whether a state is required or whether anarchy is a feasible option. The anarchist's challenge raises the question whether (i) the state can be legitimate and whether (ii) anarchy constitutes a viable practical alternative.

The normative debate about anarchy has traditionally been construed as being centred around the question whether there is any political obligation and whether states can ever be legitimate. Nozick engages with this debate but gives it a different slant. He is not primarily interested in the question as to what duties and obligations individuals have vis-à-vis the state. Rather, he inquires what the state can legitimately do to individuals. He tries to identify what the limitations on the state are and then assess whether they are so extensive as to render it incapable of existing or functioning. In other words, he takes a distinctive approach that differs markedly from the traditional discussion. His approach consists in focusing on what protective agencies are justified in doing towards individuals, rather than in assessing whether individuals have political obligations. In particular, he addresses the question as to whether these agencies can prohibit individuals from enforcing their own rights as well as from joining or forming alternative agencies. Thus, we can see that the normative issue has two aspects, one focusing on the duties of the individuals, while the other is concerned with the prerogatives of states and protective agencies.

Nozick also takes anarchism seriously as a mode of social organization. He does not dismiss the idea that an anarchical society could be a flourishing and successful society. The debate about anarchism is not just concerned with questions about rights, obligations and the legitimate use of force. It also addresses the question what the most feasible social system is to accommodate various forms of life. Nozick takes anarchism seriously as a model of society. Something very close to anarchism is considered as an ideal, a utopia towards which we should strive. Nozick does think that a minimal state is required, but he does not dismiss the possibility of a functioning anarchical system.

Within the libertarian tradition, the different sides of this debate are described as the anarchists and the minarchists. Many libertarians do acknowledge the attractiveness of anarchy, both in moral terms due to the minimization of the use of force and in social terms due to the diversity and voluntariness of social interactions. Nonetheless, many see it as not being feasible and accordingly treat government as a necessary evil. The anarchist takes a different stance and believes that governments are dispensable. He argues that a stable and peaceful system based on voluntary co-operation is possible in the absence of a state and that such a system will be preferable over other modes of social co-operation that appeal to the coercive power of the state.

This then leads to the descriptive debate about anarchy, insofar as the question arises whether anarchy can be a stable societal arrangement. The question at issue is whether anarchy is tenable or whether we will inevitably end up

with a dominant rights-enforcement agency that will hold
a monopoly of power. Here we have to assess whether
Nozick's account of the rise of the state is correct or
whether there can be a stable situation in which different
rights-enforcement agencies compete peacefully. In particular, this raises the question of the possibility of self-
enforcing mechanisms that are effective in the absence of
third-party enforcement. This is a fascinating debate, drawing on various disciplines ranging from economics to history, and no verdict has been reached yet (cf. Stringham:
2007).

Justice and entitlements

Nozick's discussion of justice is the most important part of
his work and has generated a great deal of discussion. The
arguments in favour of the entitlement theory are highly
innovative and controversial. The historical conception of
justice that Nozick develops has had an important impact.
It constitutes a radical alternative to the patterned conceptions that are so commonplace. Together with the claim
that liberty upsets patterns, this view is a serious competitor in the debate about justice. If Nozick's arguments were
to be successful, then they would undermine the vast
majority of existing conceptions of justice (since these are
patterned conceptions).

Nozick provides an insightful and helpful classification
of different conceptions of justice, distinguishing end-state
theories from (historical as well as ahistorical) patterned
accounts and contrasting them with the entitlement theory. As we saw previously, the fundamental distinction that
is to be drawn is one that distinguishes between structural
and procedural conceptions of justice. This distinction is
helpful from a taxonomical point of view, allowing us to

bundle together various conceptions of justice by identifying their fundamental characteristics. Moreover, it enables us to consider the problem of justice in holdings in terms of the generic features of differing conceptions of justice. Rather than having to assess each conception individually, we can discuss different types of theories that are characterized by certain generic features.

The main contribution that Nozick made to the debate about justice is the development of the entitlement theory and his critique of competing accounts. The entitlement theory is a radical alternative to the standard theories. Nozick has put on the table an alternative way of thinking about justice. He has put into doubt the idea that justice is a matter of patterns and that the only question is which pattern it is that needs to be implemented. Rather than considering justice as a matter of conforming to some fixed pattern, it becomes an issue of the procedures that give rise to a set of holdings.

The entitlement theory that Nozick has sketched needs to be developed, defended and elaborated. While its formal features have been clearly delimited in that it consists of three sets of principles dealing with appropriation, transfer and rectification, the details of these various principles still have to be worked out. There is a need to provide actual principles, rather than simply specify what kinds of principles are required. Moreover, there is an interesting question as to whether there are other procedural accounts that are distinct from the entitlement theory. If such conceptions should exist, the question would arise whether these accounts require a more extensive state.

In order for the entitlement theory to be viable, it must provide an adequate account of original acquisition. The account of acquisition forms the basis of the entitlement theory. As discussed above, there are a number of problems with Nozick's discussion of initial acquisition. It is not clear how entitlements to particular objects are to arise, what the extent is of the rights that are acquired in this way and what baseline should be used for assessing whether the appropriation satisfies the proviso. Though these are serious problems, it should be kept in mind that patterned conceptions are no better off in that they need to give an account of appropriation as well.

While it is in need of elaboration and while various difficulties regarding appropriation and rectification need to be dealt with, it is clear that the entitlement theory is a serious competitor in the debate about justice and that it constitutes a radical and fruitful departure from the traditional way of thinking about justice.

The argument that liberty upsets patterns and the argument that taxation on earnings from labour is on a par with forced labour have put significant pressure on patterned conceptions of justice. If successful, these arguments would show that pattern theorists are committed to restricting freedom and giving up the idea of self-ownership. The high costs of these commitments would strongly support the entitlement theory.

These two arguments identify two problematic features of pattern theories, namely that they are static and extrinsically sensitive. On the one hand, the Wilt Chamberlain example shows that pattern theorists do not leave room for change, but are rigid and static. They specify an outcome that is to be achieved, rather than a dynamic process. Once the desired pattern has been implemented, there is nothing more to do. Changes will have to be resisted since they are likely to upset the pattern. The entitlement theory, on the contrary, is a procedural account and is thereby able to accommodate change. It is essentially dynamic, specifying how distributions can be transformed in a way that is justice-preserving.

On the other hand, the forced labour analogy shows the extent to which patterned theories make the justness of a person's holdings dependent on what holdings other people have. The holdings that a person receives according to a pattern do not soley depend on his actions and interactions, but on what the social product is. Individuals receive a share of the social product, whereby their share is determined by some pattern. As a result, people have a claim on a share of the social product, even though this is the product of the work and effort of other people. This implies that patterns give individuals claims on other people. The entitlement theory, on the contrary, does not make entitlements dependent on what other people are entitled to at that time. It thereby does not give people claims on other people and is consequently compatible with self-ownership.

Both of the arguments need to be substantiated. As regards the Wilt Chamberlain example, there is the question as to what notion of freedom is at issue and to what extent a certain conception of property rights is presupposed in making the argument. If a rights-based definition of liberty is at issue and if this should presuppose an account of property rights, then the entitlement theory will wholly rest on the account of initial acquisition. Furthermore, one has to assess the costs associated with patterned accounts that go beyond the restrictions on liberty, but that derive from their static nature which requires the prohibition of mutually beneficial exchanges and which gives rise to the partially self-defeating character of pattern theories. As regards the analogy to forced labour, the question arises as to what role is to be accorded to self-ownership and as to what extent patterns give rise to claims on other people and thereby to partial ownership in other people. Moreover, there is the question whether taxation is a case of coercion equivalent to forced labour even though people can choose how much they are going to work and what kind of work they are going to do.

Nozick's discussion of the moral arbitrariness of talents and social circumstances is insightful and highly relevant to the contemporary debate about luck-egalitarianism. Rawls argued that society should be arranged in such a manner as to neutralize the morally arbitrary effects of differences in natural talents and social circumstances. This view has been adopted and worked out in much detail by a number of political theorists, resulting in a position that is described as luck-egalitarianism. This position states that morally arbitrary differences should be neutralized and that matters of brute luck should not give rise to differences in resources, welfare or well-being. Distributions should be sensitive to choices, but not to natural endowments. However, these luck-egalitarian positions developed from Rawls's starting point are equally susceptible to Nozick's challenges as the view originally propounded by Rawls himself. As we saw, Nozick distinguishes between a positive and negative argument that appeals to this kind of arbitrariness. While positive arguments are inadequate, negative arguments can be used to criticize certain patterned conceptions of justice but are ineffective against the entitlement theory.

More precisely, a positive argument attempts to establish that differences should be neutralized to the extent to which they derive from differences in natural talents and from social circumstances that are due to brute luck. This kind of argument is problematic since it presupposes a presumption in favour of equality, which is a premise that is neither defended by Rawls nor by his luck-egalitarian successors. To point out that certain differences are the results of brute luck does not in any way imply that these differences ought to be neutralized.

Given this failure to present successful positive arguments, luck-egalitarians are at best able to give negative arguments that undercut arguments in favour of differential holdings. Such negative arguments point out that differences in natural talents giving rise to differential holdings are not deserved, thereby ensuring that the differential holdings are not deserved. This then implies that arguments which try to justify differential holdings by pointing out that they are correlated with differences in talents fail. Thus, the negative arguments undercut certain patterned accounts of justice. However, these arguments are ineffective against the entitlement theory. This is because the entitlement theory is not a patterned conception of justice. It is concerned with what people are entitled to and not with what they deserve. Since we are entitled to our talents (given a commitment to self-ownership), we are entitled to the differential holdings resulting from the exercise of our talents even if these differential holdings are not deserved.

Thus, Nozick's discussion shows that the fact that certain differences are due to brute luck simply implies that these differences are neither justified nor unjustified. The differences are simply a matter of luck and there is nothing about luck per se that implies that it should be eradicated or that differences resulting therefrom should be neutralized. An independent argument to the effect that luck should be neutralized is required to justify redistribution.

More precisely, an argument would have to be given that shows that holdings should be patterned in a luck-insensitive manner. Such an argument would have to establish that all differences could only be legitimate to the extent to which they are deserved. This kind of patterned account, however, is subject to Nozick's critiques and the luck-egalitarian arguments are ineffective against the entitlement view.

The meta-utopia

Nozick's account of the framework for utopia as an inspiring ideal of libertarianism has been much neglected. Nonetheless, it contains important insights and is highly interesting and original. Two aspects of this discussion, in particular, are of lasting relevance and import, namely his attempt to (i) identify a realistic libertarian utopia that consists in a meta-utopia and to (ii) develop a framework that respects the diversity of people and renders the non-coercive pursuit of differing utopian conceptions compatible.

Nozick recognizes the importance of providing a positive vision that goes beyond the negative injunction not to violate rights and not to expand the minimal state. Libertarianism is not only morally right but also inspiring. As Nozick argues, libertarianism promises more than just being the most efficient system. It promises even more than being the only morally justified political arrangement. In addition to these important considerations, it is also a highly inspiring vision of society. It is an ideal towards which we should strive.

Showing the ways in which the minimal state is inspiring and how it constitutes an ideal towards which we should strive is an important task. While being utopian, Nozick's positive view has the advantage of being realistic as well, insofar as it is a meta-utopia that is not based on the problematic assumptions of particular utopian visions. In this way it is a distinctively non-utopian utopia. It thereby manages to combine the appeal and attractiveness deriving from particular utopian schemes, without suffering from their impracticality and lack of realism.

The framework for utopia shows that there is more to libertarianism than a critique of government. It shows that there is an inspiring positive understanding of society and of human interactions. This meta-utopia is one that can be shared by many people precisely because it is a framework for utopia that allows the flourishing of different non-coercive forms of life. It is not just a negative political philosophy that tries to place constraints on the state. It also contains a distinctive positive vision of what a good society would look like. What makes it peculiar and differentiates it from other utopian ideals is that it is a framework for utopia. It is not a dogmatic and fixed conception of how things should be done that needs to be imposed on those who hold different conceptions of the good. Instead, it is flexible and can be embraced by different people that have different conceptions of what counts as a good life.

This ideal does not describe a particular society and does not specify particular social relations. Instead, it is concerned with the structural features of the society. The libertarian cannot and does not want to give a blue-print for society. He does not want to specify a pattern to which society has to conform. He does not make detailed claims about how things will work out or how they should work out. Instead, the particularities are left to spontaneous social forces. The ideal society is specified by a process that satisfies certain structural constraints, rather than being specified by some pattern or end-state. The ideal society is the outcome of the voluntary and peaceful actions and interactions of different individuals.

These structural constraints place substantive constraints on actions and thereby place restrictions on ways of life. In particular, the framework for utopia rules out the implementation of imperialistic utopian visions by means of coercion, i.e. the coercive imposition of utopian conceptions onto others. As a result of these structural features, the meta-utopian vision is substantive enough to allow for criticisms of coercive ways of life. It provides a standard by means of which we can assess different conceptions of the good and which allows us to rule out the coercive imposition onto others as being impermissible. This feature of the framework for utopia gives it a distinctive advantage over other libertarian accounts, such as Kukathas's ideal of a liberal archipelago, which lack the resources to criticize coercive conceptions of the good. Accordingly, the meta-utopia allows us to provide an inspiring vision of society that is appealing to people holding different conceptions of the good, while at the same time being sufficiently substantive to rule out coercive utopian practices.

The flexible nature of the meta-utopia leads us to the second noteworthy aspect of Nozick's account, namely the importance of dealing with differing conceptions of the good. The framework for utopia is compatible with a broad range of differing conceptions of the good. This view of the good society takes seriously the diversity and individuality of different people. This is especially important in heterogeneous societies, such as in multicultural societies, where there are significant differences between the value systems of different individuals. The framework for utopia is a framework within which these different conceptions of the good can peacefully co-exist and flourish.

The compatibility with a large number of differing utopian schemes, namely all those that are not coercive, is advantageous in several respects. First of all, it allows everyone to try to pursue his vision of what the best life is for him. No one is forced to live a life he does not want to live. No one is forced to accept a certain value system. Accordingly, the diversity and individuality of different people can be accommodated by a diversity of ways of life.

Second, as Nozick argues, we can show that the framework for utopia is a great filter device for identifying and testing conceptions of the good. That is, we can give Millian arguments about the instrumental value of freedom and diversity. If everyone can freely choose how to live his life, then it is likely that there will be many experiments in living. No static order will be imposed. Instead, different ways of life will be tried out. Some of them will flourish, while others will perish. Conceptions of the good will be subjected to trial and error, allowing people to experiment and discover, to learn and imitate.

Third, while Nozick does not make use of moral considerations to argue in favour of his meta-utopia, we can note that the framework is inspiring because it is a non-coercive and non-paternalistic system that is characterized by a high degree of tolerance. It respects the autonomy of individuals (as long as they do not interfere with the autonomy of others). It allows people to pursue their conception of the good. It lets them do what they think is best. It thereby treats them as rational and autonomous agents.

While the structure of the framework for utopia is clear, many problems need to be addressed and various details still need to be worked out. In particular, there is the problem

of motivating the idea that we should be neutral between
different conceptions of the good, as well as the closely
related problem of justifying the prohibition on the coercive pursuit of utopian visions. Additionally, there are many
issues pertaining to the implementation of the framework
for utopia. For example, it is unclear whether the framework requires us to make people accept values associated
with the minimal state, notably property rights and freedom of choice, and what should be done about conceptions of the good that are explicitly anti-capitalistic but yet
non-coercive. Are they not coerced by the meta-utopia to
accept capitalistic norms and values embodied by the
minimal state? Then there are problems relating to transaction costs involved in moving from one association to
another, issues pertaining to the availability of information
about alternative associations, problems pertaining to the
existence of a real exit option and the possibility of imposing costs on members to discourage them from exiting
associations, as well as issues about educating children and
ensuring that they can voluntarily choose which association
to join. Moreover, there is a question of how far tolerance
should go, for example whether associations countenanc-
ing voluntary slavery should be tolerated.

The framework for utopia is a realistic meta-utopia. It is
utopian in the positive sense of being an inspiring ideal
towards which we should strive. It is an ideal of the best
possible world for each of us. At the same time it is not
utopian in the negative sense of being unrealistic and
hopelessly idealistic. This is because the implementation
of the framework does not require the conversion of large
segments of mankind. It is not necessary to overcome various obstacles, whether they regard the moral character or
education of the people or whether certain technological

progress needs to be previously achieved. Moreover, it does not need a radical reshaping of society but can be achieved in a piecemeal manner. The minimal state can be achieved by gradually minimizing the state, rather than requiring a wholesale revolutionary modification of social and political structures. That being said, there are nonetheless obstacles towards the establishment of the minimal state and utopia cannot be gained cheaply but requires social and political activism in order to overcome vested interests.

The framework for utopia thus exhibits an interesting and fruitful combination of realism, radicalism and utopianism. It is based on realistic assumptions about the diversity and individuality of different people. Accordingly, it does not make implausible assumptions about human nature. At the same time, it is radical since it implies a conception of society that is fundamentally at odds with ours. Significant changes will be required, if the framework for utopia is to be realized in practice. Moreover, it is utopian in the sense of being an idealistic and inspiring vision that captures the idea of being the best possible world for each of us.

Bibliography

Barnett, R. E. (1977), 'Whither anarchy: has Robert Nozick justified the state?' *Journal of Libertarian Studies*, 1 (1), pp. 15–21.

Cohen, G. A. (1995), *Self-Ownership, Freedom, and Equality*. Cambridge: Cambridge University Press.

Davis, L. (1981), 'Nozick's entitlement theory', in J. Paul (ed.), *Reading Nozick: Essays on Anarchy, State, and Utopia*. Totowa, NJ: Rowman & Littlefield Publishers, pp. 344–354.

Hailwood, S. A. (1996), *Exploring Nozick: Beyond Anarchy, State, and Utopia*. Aldershot: Avebury.

Holmes, R. (1981), 'Nozick on anarchism', in J. Paul (ed.), *Reading Nozick: Essays on Anarchy, State, and Utopia*. Totowa, NJ: Rowman & Littlefield Publishers, pp. 57–67.

Kukathas, C. and Pettit, P. (1990), *Rawls: A Theory of Justice and Its Critics*. Stanford, CA: Stanford University Press.

Long, R. T. (2002), 'Robert Nozick, philosopher of liberty'. *The Freeman: Ideas on Liberty*, 52 (9), pp. 30–33.

Lyons, D. (1981), 'The new Indian claims and original rights to land', in J. Paul (ed.), *Reading Nozick: Essays on Anarchy, State, and Utopia*. Totowa, NJ: Rowman & Littlefield Publishers, pp. 355–379.

Mack, E. (1975), 'Review of *Anarchy, State, and Utopia*'. *Reason Magazine*, November 1975, pp. 6–12.

—(1981), 'Nozick on unproductivity: the unintended consequences', in J. Paul (ed.), *Reading Nozick: Essays on Anarchy, State, and Utopia*. Totowa, NJ: Rowman & Littlefield Publishers, pp. 169–190.

—(2002), 'Self-ownership, Marxism, and egalitarianism – Part 1: challenges to historical entitlement'. *Politics, Philosophy, and Economics*, 1 (1), pp. 75–108.

Miller, D. (2002), 'The justification of political authority', in D. Schmidtz (ed.), *Robert Nozick*. Cambridge: Cambridge University Press, pp. 10–33.

Nagel, T. (1981), 'Libertarianism without foundations', in J. Paul (ed.), *Reading Nozick: Essays on Anarchy, State, and Utopia.* Totowa, NJ: Rowman & Littlefield Publishers, pp. 191–205.

Nozick, R. (1974), *Anarchy, State, and Utopia.* New York: Basic Books.

—(1981), *Philosophical Explanations.* Cambridge, MA: Harvard University Press.

—(1989), *The Examined Life: Philosophical Meditations.* New York: Simon & Schuster.

—(1993), *The Nature of Rationality.* Princeton, NJ: Princeton University Press.

—(1997), *Socratic Puzzles.* Cambridge, MA: Harvard University Press.

—(2001), *Invariances: The Structure of the Objective World.* Cambridge, MA: Harvard University Press.

O'Neill, O. (1981), 'Nozick's entitlements', in J. Paul (ed.), *Reading Nozick: Essays on Anarchy, State, and Utopia.* Totowa, NJ: Rowman & Littlefield Publishers, pp. 305–322.

Paul, J. (1981), 'The withering of Nozick's minimal state', in J. Paul (ed.), *Reading Nozick: Essays on Anarchy, State, and Utopia.* Totowa, NJ: Rowman & Littlefield Publishers, pp. 68–76.

Pogge, T. (1989), *Realizing Rawls.* Ithaca, NY: Cornell University Press.

Rawls, J. (1971), *A Theory of Justice.* Cambridge, MA: Harvard University Press.

—(1977), 'The basic structure as subject'. *American Philosophical Quarterly,* 14 (2), pp. 159–165.

Ryan, C. C. (1981), 'Yours, mine, and ours: property rights and individual liberty', in J. Paul (ed.), *Reading Nozick: Essays on Anarchy, State, and Utopia.* Totowa, NJ: Rowman & Littlefield Publishers, pp. 323–343.

Scheffler, S. (1981), 'Natural rights, equality, and the minimal state', in J. Paul (ed.), *Reading Nozick: Essays on Anarchy, State, and Utopia.* Totowa, NJ: Rowman & Littlefield Publishers, pp. 148–168.

Schmidtz, D. (2005), 'History and pattern', in E. F. Paul, F. D. Miller and J. Paul (eds), *Natural Rights Liberalism from Locke to Nozick.* Cambridge: Cambridge University Press, pp. 148–177.

Singer, P. (1981), 'The right to be rich or poor', in J. Paul (ed.), *Reading Nozick: Essays on Anarchy, State, and Utopia.* Totowa, NJ: Rowman & Littlefield Publishers, pp. 37–53.

Steiner, H. (1977), '*Anarchy, State, and Utopia*: book review'. *Mind*, 86 (341), pp. 120–129.

Stringham, E. (2007), *Anarchy and the Law*. New Brunswick, NY: Transaction Publishers.

Tuck, R. (1979), *Natural Rights Theories: Their Origin and Development*. Cambridge: Cambridge University Press.

Waldron, J. (1982), 'Ours by right: review of *Reading Nozick*'. *Times Literary Supplement*, 19th November 1982, p. 1277.

—(2005), 'Nozick and Locke: filling the space of rights', in E. F. Paul, F. D. Miller and J. Paul (eds), *Natural Rights Liberalism from Locke to Nozick*. Cambridge: Cambridge University Press, pp. 81–110.

Wolff, J. (1991), *Robert Nozick: Property, Justice, and the Minimal State*. Stanford, CA: Stanford University Press.

Index